Simple Folk
Instruments to

Ilene Hunter &
Marilyn Judson

Make and to Play

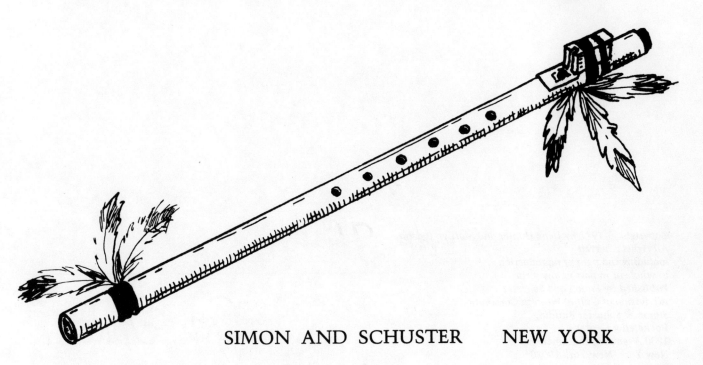

SIMON AND SCHUSTER   NEW YORK

Published by Simon and Schuster
A Division of Gulf & Western Corporation
Simon & Schuster Building
Rockefeller Center
1230 Avenue of the Americas
New York, New York 10020

Designed by Elizabeth Woll
Manufactured in the United States of America

1   2   3   4   5   6   7   8   9   10

Library of Congress Cataloging in Publication Data

Hunter, Ilene.
  Simple folk instruments to make and play.

  Bibliography: p.
  1. Musical instruments—Construction.   I. Judson,
Marilyn, joint author.   II. Title.
ML460.H9   781.9'1   76-50091

ISBN 0-671-22446-8

781.91
H

Contents

ACKNOWLEDGMENTS

We wish to extend our warmest thanks to—

—our husbands, Bob and Charles, who encouraged not only this book but our individuality and ability as women.

—Ireane Peggs, for sharing the experiences of her years as a musician and Girl Scout leader.

—Charles Judson, for his fine photography and his time.

—Mary Aspaas for her enthusiastic response.

—our children who greeted the project with enthusiasm and helped in many ways.

—Julie Houston, our editor, for her encouragement and great humor.

Washtub Bass, Dulcimer and Bamboo Flute played by Todd Judson, Joanne Hunter and Janet Hunter.

Response to music is innate in all people and the joy of musical creation should not be limited to professional musicians.

'Tis a gift to be simple,
'Tis a gift to be free,
'Tis a gift to come down where
    you ought to be.
And when you are in the place
    just right
You'll be in the valley of love
    and delight.

—From a hymn of the Shakers, who felt that music was one of the keys to salvation.

About Music and Instruments

What was the first song? We will never know because a melody can't sink into a tar pit, nor can it be carved upon a cave wall. It must be created anew each time.

Primitive man found that music, whether it was the imitation of a bird song or the re-creation of a bison hunt, gave him a feeling of control over the dark world beyond his campfire. He added simple instruments to his song and these are still found today as basic elements of his religion. The Jewish rabbi blows a shofar (ram's horn); the Indian medicine man beats his drum; and the Christian priest rings a bell in the church steeple.

Twentieth-century instruments are very complex. The electronic inventions have created new areas of specialization, but the human body and human emotions have not changed. Man still needs to express himself physically; sound and rhythm must be re-created and adjusted to heartbeats and social needs. Small children who dance and play rhythm instruments have smiles on their faces showing the special relationship of music, dance and emotion.

Ilene's interest in the different ways of producing music came from a childhood spent on an Apache Indian reservation, hearing Apache music as well as the songs of other Arizona Indian tribes. Later, as an adult musician and teacher, it was not difficult for her to realize that all folk songs express the same human thoughts and emotions although their notes may be different.

The artistry of music is also expressed in the construction and appearance of the instrument. Primitive musicians were also craftsmen. Marilyn's ability as an artist and a craftswoman helped to translate the musical ideas into tangible form, and then to put these forms onto paper.

All the instruments in this book may be constructed with simple tools and may be used by people of all ages. Some of the string instruments are harder to construct, but we have made simplified versions for children in addition to the more difficult types that require the steady hands of adults.

The book is arranged to follow the popular division of instruments into percussion, string and wind sections. Many of the instruments have been singled out for special ethnic groups. Each section ends with a page entitled "Quick and Simple." These are sound producers that can be found around the house and constructed in a few minutes.

There are two additional sections that we hope will contribute to the use of this book. One section has suggestions for teachers and recreation directors, and the other gives methods for construction and for working with different materials.

We hope you will adapt the ideas in this book to your own individual needs and interests. Music still needs to be created anew by each person for, like primitive man, we all still find shadows beyond the firelight.

Suggestions for Teachers and Recreation Leaders

How many ways can you make music without an instrument? Of course you can sing and whistle, but what else can you do? You can clap with your hands: the Genteel Lady clap, quiet and soft with the fingers of one hand in the palm of the other; the Congratulations clap, sharp and crisp with flat hands together; or the Oh Wow clap, loud and resonant with cupped hands. Besides these, you can pat your knees, slap your thighs, tap your toes and click your heels. Your whole body provides a lot of simple folk instruments!

The spirit of music, the re-creation, the personal involvement gets lost in these days of television, radio and quadraphonic sound. We mouth the maxim that small children require rhythm band instruments, but adults need involvement as much as children. An old spiritual says, "All God's Chillun Got a Song." We don't need to wait for heaven to put on our wings and sing a bit.

There are many ways in which the instruments in this book can be used. Some of the suggestions that follow may help you adapt them for your personal needs.

SMALL CHILDREN—PRESCHOOL, EARLY ELEMENTARY SCHOOL

Very young children lack the coordination necessary for detailed construction, but if the teacher makes a few preparations beforehand, the children will be able to do simple sawing, sanding, and painting. The first two sections of our book, Rhythm Sticks and Rasps, and Jingle Bells and Rattles, will provide good rhythm instruments for children of this age. The Quick and Simple pages of all sections are suitable for young children. Elementary school children will be able to make most of the instruments with a little guidance.

Teachers who use the Orf-Schulwerk method with its emphasis on rhythm, verse and creativity may want to add some of these instruments to the beautiful but expensive Orf instruments. In this way each child can have several instruments from which to choose. Instruments using a pentatonic scale are often more easily constructed than purchased.

SUMMER CAMPS, RECREATION CENTERS

Groups which have more time for projects will find that beginning musicians can construct their instruments, begin rehearsals and pre-

sent a music program on the same day. The new instruments can accompany singing or be used with a record player. Tape recorders provide a way of taking music to a far corner of the playground or camp for any group that wants to rehearse or perform in private.

A section with trees can be designated as a Sound Center. Bells and gongs as well as slit drums and wooden xylophones can be hung from trees. A long glass-bottle xylophone may be also strung between two trees.

For hiking or back-packing trips the small zanza or shepherd's pipe can be put in a pack without adding much weight. At the campsite, an original washtub bass can be constructed with a string, a sheet of plastic and a hole in the ground. Small rocks will make Hawaiian castanets and a wood rasp can be cut and played on the bottom of a kettle. The section on drums has other suggestions for group participation. This is the type of music that nomadic people have used throughout history.

MUSIC CLASSES

Teachers have found that the use of rhythm instruments facilitates the learning of the rhythmic systems of notation used in Western music. The Haydn Toy Symphony has notations for bird whistles, bells, etc.

The study of musical notation is often difficult for children and adults because the five-line staff looks like a strange puzzle. The small zither can be used to demonstrate the ladderlike simplicity of the staff. Instead of a triangular sound box, make the instrument on a small board. First paint a large staff on the board, then position the strings so that each one can be tuned to the line or space directly below it. Students can then play the note and see how it is written at the same time. Commercial zithers are available with sheets of paper that slide under the strings and show which strings to pluck to make a tune. Each student can make his own music paper for his instrument.

Xylophones and similar instruments must be tuned accurately. If you don't have skill or a good piano to help, you should ask a musical friend for aid.

Instruments tuned in the same five-tone scale can be played in unison by amateurs. When shakers and drums are added to these instruments some exciting orchestral results are possible.

For those who can ignore Western tradition, some of the instruments, especially the flutes, can be tuned in a casual manner by just making the finger holes that suit your fingers. This makes the flute one of a kind, an individual instrument, but naturally it cannot be played in unison with other flutes.

Stringed instruments may also be tuned to your liking. A simple way for a two-stringed instrument is to tune both strings to the same tone; finger just one string and leave the second as a drone. The Appalachian dulcimer follows this principle—the strings are tuned to different notes for different songs. Some dulcimer players follow a more complicated system. The books recommended in the reference section give very good directions for playing and tuning this instrument. Teachers will find that this type of tuning gives new insight into the different musical modes.

ETHNIC STUDIES

The basic methods of producing sound are similar the world around, and teachers will find that slight variations in the construction and decoration of an instrument will make it represent different originals. For example, gourd rattles are found everywhere in the warmer latitudes. The same gourd (or one of the substitutes we have listed) may be decorated with feathers and become a Hawaiian uli-uli; with buckskin ties it can be an American Indian shaker; with bright paint it will resemble a Mexican maraca; with a brown design or a woodburning kit it will become an African rattle.

Stringed instruments are very adaptable. The banjo has one open side on the sound box. The Russian balalaika has a partially closed triangular resonator, while the Spanish guitar has a pear-shaped one. All have a long neck and strings in common. The rawhide violin we have shown can be made into a plucked instrument, or it can be made to resemble a spike fiddle from Arabia or Cambodia and played between the knees. For detailed pictures of folk instruments, see Folk Music Instruments of the World by A. Buchner, or other books listed in the reference section.

We have shown instruments from many cultures, including Hawaiian, Indian, African and Mexican. For example, from Hawaii we have shown the uli-uli, pu-ili and ili-ili. The conch shell horn could be used with these, as could the Philippine tinakling poles. These can be used with ukuleles or guitars and traditional songs. A teacher who wants to be creative with a sense of humor can change the bleach bottle banjo into a ukulele by using a dishwashing detergent bottle placed sideways on a short wooden neck.

American Indian music is well represented here. There are different rattles, clappers, and drums as well as a flute and a bone whistle. See References for more about Indian music and dancing—several books are listed.

African basket rattles, gourd rattles, musical bows, zanzas and drums are shown. Mexican maracas, guiros, claves and rasps are also listed. Many instruments of both these ethnic groups have come from south of the border where instruments used before the coming of Columbus have been adapted and changed by the Spanish, Portuguese, and Africans who settled there many centuries ago. Included in the *reference section is a book on the making of steel drums, if you think you can withstand the noise required in making them.*

All of these cultures have come together in the United States, the melting pot of the world. But the country is a mere two hundred years old, and its musical instruments still reflect the homelands of the immigrants. One striking aspect of music is its relationship to early childhood experiences. Most people have heard their favorite song during childhood or adolescence. Modern symphony orchestras disappoint their audiences if they do not replay eighteenth-century favorites every year. Our favorite Christmas music comes from the sixteenth, seventeenth, and eighteenth centuries. The "new" music is actively disliked by a large part of our population.

When the different national groups arrived in pioneer settlements, they carried little extra baggage. As time permitted, they re-created musical instruments and songs remembered from childhood, then they added a few extras that they had heard while traveling. American folk music reflects their experiences. Settlers in the Appalachian Mountains, for example, took the five-tone Scotch bagpipe scale, mixed it with the rhythmicity of the Spanish guitar and the African banjo, and came up with songs like "Old Joe Clark," "Mary Had a Little Lamb," and "Amazing Grace." Another corner of the land combined the ballads with rhythm to create a whole new sound, that of New Orleans jazz. Two books by Bruno Nettl (see References) give more information on the historical development of American folk music.

DANCING

Dancing and music are considered the same in many parts of the world. Responding to rhythm with your body is part of the art of making music. Many of these instruments are intended to be used by dancers and there are many variations.

Small children will especially enjoy making the paper plate tambourines. Girls will like the wire hoops (any size) of bells and flowers for folk dances from Mexico, England and Poland. The colorful circles can be shared with a partner, twirled over one arm, or worn on the head like a flower wreath. Boys especially enjoy dancing with feathered rattles and American Indian drums.

Directions for dancing with the tinakling poles may be found in Songs in Action *by P. Gelineau, and in other books on folk dancing.*

Styles of Indian dancing vary greatly in all parts of the United States. There are many books with photographs and directions that can help you keep your presentation accurate.

SCIENCE CLASSES

There is much demonstration material here for the study of sound waves and vibrations. A stringed instrument can be made on a single stick or a curved back like the Chinese "chin." This stringed stick can then be set over different resonators to show the contrast in sound.

Horns and whistles show the characteristics of wind currents, and the problems of making a whistle blow make these elements very clear.

Musical glasses and panpipes demonstrate the effects of size, shape and depth upon tones as the human ear hears them.

A simple toy which shows the effects of vibrations can be made by fastening a small propeller (part of an ice cream stick) on the end of a rasp. When the rasp is rubbed the propeller will turn according to the direction of the rubbing.

FINAL CONSIDERATIONS

No sounds from a plastic bottle or a plain box can hope to equal the clear mellow tones of a professionally constructed instrument. All children and adults who love music enough to spend time in practicing should use a good quality instrument. We hope that some people who start with these easy ones will advance to the more complex instruments, which will reward their efforts and hours of study with the satisfactions experienced by skilled creative artists. But, for all others who enjoy folk music, we hope this book will offer ways of participating in the simple re-creation of music—your own music.

Methods and Materials

Most of the instruments in this book can be made with the minimum of equipment.

EQUIPMENT

The pieces of equipment used for building these instruments are those in the basic home workshop: hammer, pliers, saw (coping or electric), screwdriver, drill (hand or electric), etc.

The other items—such as dowels, wood, sandpaper, nails, screw eyes, etc.—can be purchased at the local hardware store. We have found that these stores are very cooperative and will often cut your wood, drill a hole and give good advice when you are constructing these instruments.

Strings and machined heads for guitars, banjos or violins can be either purchased or ordered from a music store. Craft shops or art stores are the places to purchase rawhide, leather, or the Mexican self-hardening clay.

SELECTING AND PREPARING BRANCHES (for drumsticks, rasps and bows)

A hardwood branch (such as birch or maple) is the best for drumsticks, rasps and bows, since these will not split as easily as the soft woods will. For any of these uses, the branch should be straight for the desired length.

The size of the branch depends on the item you are making. Drumsticks should be ½" in diameter, rasps ⅝" to 1½" in diameter, and bows about ⅜" in diameter. The lengths vary from 8" to 24".

When you have found a branch that is the desired diameter and length, peel off the bark with a knife. If you are making a bow or a drum rattle stick, bend the branch (while green) to the shape desired and secure by tying or taping. Dry in this position. Drying the branches may take several days or a week, depending on the weather. The branch is dry when it will retain the desired shape.

When the branch is dry, sand and finish with wax or stain.

SELECTING AND DRYING GOURDS

Gourds should be selected for size according to the instrument you are making. To remove membrane and seeds, cut the gourd with a knife in a spot where you will be able to slip a long-handled spoon in to scrape the membrane and seeds loose. (If you are making a gourd rattle and want the seeds for the noisemaker, save and dry them.)

Dry the gourd in the sun or in a dry warm spot in the house. This can take from two days to two weeks, depending on your climate. To dry rapidly you may place the gourd in the oven overnight at a very low temperature—150°—or over a furnace vent.

SELECTING, CUTTING AND DRYING COCONUTS

Coconuts are available in most grocery stores. The largest in our area was 5" in diameter.

Draining the coconut is simple. At one end (the stem end) you will find three indentations. Take an ice pick or sharp instrument and poke a hole in each indentation. Alternatively, use a drill to make the holes. Set on end and drain. When drained, saw through the coconut; if you have a vise you can put the coconut in it to hold it firm while sawing. Cut the coconut according to the instrument you are making.

Place the coconut in the sun or a warm, low-temperature oven to dry. Remove the meat when it shrinks from the shell and proceed with your instrument.

MAKING PAPIER MÂCHÉ

Papier mâché is a very inexpensive way to create an instrument. We used it mainly for rattles, but with a little imagination you could use it for the base of many of the instruments, such as the tambourine, or the Apache rattle (in place of fabric); it can also be used for decorating instruments.

Tearing the newspaper rather than cutting it gives a feathered edge. The soft edge laps more evenly, and this makes your finished product smoother and easier to decorate.

If white glue is used, dilute it with an equal amount of water. If you prefer to use the flour and water method, put the flour in a bowl and add just enough water to make a paste. Be sure it is not too runny. Beat the mixture with a spoon until smooth. Wallpaper paste may also be used, following the directions on the package.

Dip the torn pieces of newspaper in the glue or paste, one piece at a time, and lay them over the item you are using for a base (balloon, light bulb, etc.). Cover the object completely with at least four layers of the papier mâché—the more layers the stronger the instrument.

Hang the papier mâché piece in a warm place to dry. Drying time depends on your climate and the number of layers of paper used.

STIFFENING FABRIC FOR RATTLES

We found you can make a nice rattle or drumhead from fabric. Dip cotton fabric in a solution of three parts white glue and one part water and let the fabric dry overnight (lay it over a bowl or something else in the shape you desire). The fabric will be hard and the sound of the noisemakers hitting it is satisfactory.

CUTTING TIN

"Tin" from food cans provides another material for making musical instruments.

Cut the can with tinsnips, being very careful not to cut yourself on the metal, and open flat. (To prevent cuts, wear gloves.) Draw the shape you are interested in making on the tin with a grease pencil, and cut it out with the tinsnips. Pliers are best for bending the metal into the shape you desire.

PAPER FLOWERS

These are used for decorating the instruments. Paper flowers may be purchased at craft stores or specialty houses or they can be made. Making them is a great way to utilize the colored tissue from gifts. Cut strips of tissue 2" x 4" and layer three or more strips; twist the center with floral wire or tape and you have a colorful and decorative flower.

LAMINATING CARDBOARD

Cardboard cartons are readily available and very inexpensive. Cut three or four squares of cardboard the size of the item you wish to make. Apply white glue between each layer, dry thoroughly, and you have a very strong, thick piece of board to work with. Draw the shape you want and cut it out with a knife—or you can use a saw.

DRILLING HOLES IN SHELLS AND ROCKS

If available, use an electric drill; this makes the drilling go faster, especially if you have many shells or rocks to drill. This can be done with a hand drill. A carbide bit is best for either hand or electric drill. Place the bit on the rock or shell and make a small indentation where the hole is to be—this gives you a firm place to put the bit—then gently but firmly make your hole.

STRINGS

For stringed instruments we found that nylon fishing line is very good. We strongly recommend the heavy test strength, such as 25-pound, which is strong and safer than lighter line for pulling taut. Strings for instruments that you are making can be purchased at music stores, or you can use old strings from guitars, banjos and dulcimers.

RAWHIDE

Rawhide for drums is fun to work with and the results are exciting. Place pieces of it in cool water until soft, and stretch over or around the frame while wet. Tie or tack it in place and let it dry thoroughly. Rawhide is very flexible while wet and becomes very stiff and taut when dry.

BELLS

Ready-made bells may be purchased in many qualities. Variety stores carry inexpensive, thin-sounding ones. Craft shops and import stores offer bells with more musical tones.

Rhythm Sticks and Rasps

History

Did primitive men first beat time to their songs with wooden sticks? Probably, because around the world every culture has used and still uses wooden rhythm sticks as a basic instrument. Musicians have discovered that different types of wood make different sounds. They have also found ways to amplify the sounds with round amplifiers derived from the hollow log and the overturned gourd.

Rasps of many types are used for rhythmic sounds. Notching different sticks and rubbing them together gives a new rhythm for dancing. American Indians use a unique rasp in their Bear Dance. The notched sticks are played over a metal sheet which covers a hole in the ground. The resulting growl re-creates the angry spirit of a charging bear.

Rasps made from the jawbones of animals have been used in many cultures. It is only a short step from the scraping of animal teeth to the scraping of teeth carved on a long gourd. The hollow interior of the gourd gives the Mexican guiro a resonating chamber of air to magnify the tone.

California Indians have an unusual instrument called a pak'papa, a long hollow elderberry branch that makes a soft clacking sound.

There is no size limit to rhythm sticks. There are tiny finger castanets and there are giant poles used by the Philippine Islanders in their Tinakling Dance. The long sticks gently tap together as the dancers step in and out, imitating the long-legged crane that feeds among the windswept reeds of the marsh.

Rhythm Sticks

Children's rhythm bands use these sticks as a standard item in the same way that adult marching bands use the clicking drumsticks.

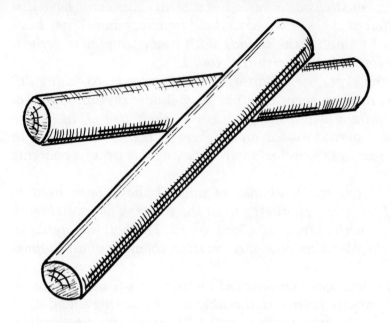

MATERIALS

1″ dowels, 12″ long, or branches from a tree. Select branches for straightness and size and hardness of wood.
Saw
Sandpaper
Shellac, varnish or paint for the finish

TO MAKE

1. Cut dowels or branches (A) to a 12″ length.
2. Sand rough edges of dowel with sandpaper. For branches, peel off bark, then sand with sandpaper.
3. Shellac or paint to give a nice finish.

TO PLAY

Hold one stick in each hand. Tap together to the beat of the music.

HINTS

Plastic or metal rods can also be used. Adjust length for the sound you wish: Starting with 12″ sticks, test the sound by hitting them together. Longer sticks will produce a lower tone, and shorter sticks a higher one.

A

Claves

Shorter and heavier than the preceding rhythm sticks, the claves are traditionally used to provide the syncopation in Latin rhythms.

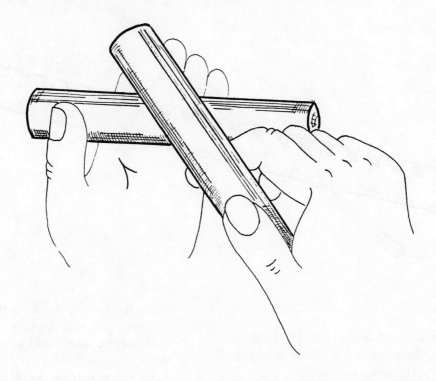

MATERIALS

2 dowels, 4″ to 8″ long by 1″ in diameter
Saw
Sandpaper

TO MAKE

1. Cut dowels (or material you choose) to lengths desired. Different lengths make different sounds.
2. Sand the rough edges.
3. Traditionally these sticks are decorated with a dark stain and bright accents.

TO PLAY

Hold one stick in a cupped left hand. This provides a miniature sounding chamber. Strike firmly with the other stick (see diagram).

HINTS

Hardwood sticks, heavy bamboo, broomsticks, plastic or metal rods may also be used.

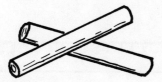

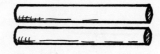

Rasp

Many shapes are possible. A Northwest Indian tribe uses a fish-shaped rasp to insure a good salmon catch.

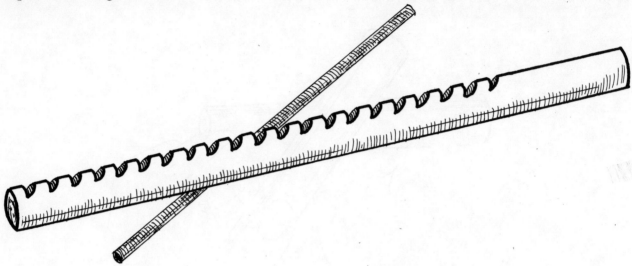

MATERIALS

2 dowels, one 1″ in diameter by 12″ long, the other ¼″ in diameter by 8″ long, or natural wood sticks of the same sizes
Saw (a coping saw will work nicely)
Pocketknife
Pencil
Sandpaper

TO MAKE

1. With the saw, cut the dowels to the proper lengths—12″ for 1″-diameter dowel and 8″ for the ¼″ dowel.

2. With the pencil, mark on the 12″ dowel every ⅜″ from one end, leaving about 4″ for holding on to at the other end (A).
3. With the saw, cut straight down into dowel ⅜″ at the pencil marks (B).
4. Notch in a "V" with the pocketknife ³⁄₁₆″ from each sawed cut (C).
5. Sand rough edges.

TO PLAY

Rub the 8″ dowel along the notched dowel.

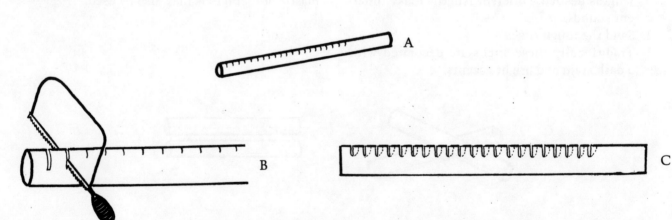

Sioux Indian Rasp

The growl of an angry bear is imitated by the Sioux Indians for their Bear Dance by rubbing a short heavy rasp with another heavy stick. The sounding chamber may be an overturned washtub or a hole in the ground covered with a metal sheet.

MATERIALS

1 dowel, 1½″ in diameter by 10″ long
1 dowel, 1″ in diameter by 10″ long
Saw
Pencil
Sandpaper

TO MAKE

1. Cut both pieces of doweling to a length of 10″.
2. With a pencil mark the 1½″-diameter dowel at ⅜″ intervals from one end, leaving 2½″ for a handle at the other end (A).

3. With a coping saw, cut "V" shapes ⅜″ deep at every other mark so that the "V" shapes will be ⅜″ apart and ⅜″ wide at the top (B).
4. Smooth rough edges with sandpaper.

TO PLAY

Hold notched stick in place on metal sheet or turned-over tub and stroke with the other, smooth dowel (see diagram).

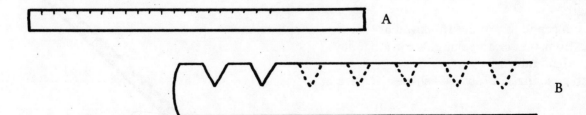

Yaqui Indian Raspador

This long notched rasp uses half a gourd or a coconut shell as a resonator. The Indian musicians sit cross-legged on a smooth tile floor as they make the crisp, hollow rhythm for the traditional Deer Dance.

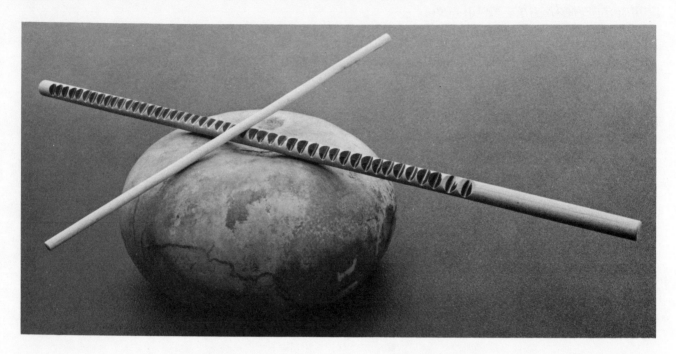

MATERIALS

1 dowel, ½" in diameter by 15" long
1 dowel, ¼" in diameter by 12" long
Pocketknife
Sandpaper
Pencil
Gourd half or coconut shell half

TO MAKE

1. Prepare gourd or coconut shell—see Methods and Materials section on how to do this.
2. With saw, cut each dowel to the proper length.
3. With a pencil, mark the 15" dowel at ½" intervals from one end, leaving 3" for a handle at the other end (A).
4. With a coping saw, cut "V" shapes ¼" deep at every other mark so that the "V" shapes will be ¼" apart and ¼" wide at the top (B).
5. Smooth rough edges with sandpaper.

TO PLAY

Place the gourd, hollow side down, on the tile floor. Hold one end of the notched rasp in one hand and lay the other end across the gourd. Rub the smooth dowel back and forth across the notches rapidly and rhythmically. An upturned washbasin will make a noisy substitute for the gourd.

A

B

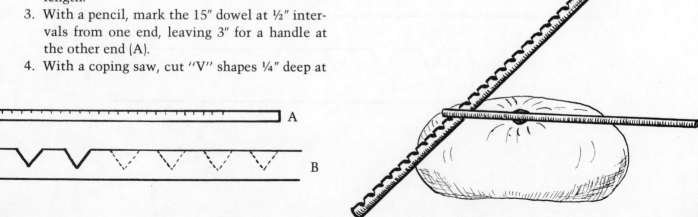

Jawbone Rasp

A real bear jaw was sometimes used by the Indians for their Bear Dance (see Sioux Indian Rasp). In Latin America and in Africa the jawbone of a donkey was used. If you happen upon a cow or horse skeleton in a field, find the jawbone and you have a ready-made instrument.

MATERIALS

Jawbone of a large animal with teeth intact (A)
Small animal bone (B)
Paints in bright colors (optional)

TO PLAY

The jawbone comes ready to play—just rub across the teeth with the small bone.

TO MAKE

1. Clean the jawbone, if necessary.
2. Paint the bones with bright colors, if desired.

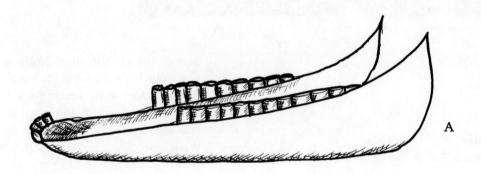

Mexican Gourd Guiro

One Latin American musician made his version from an empty artillery shell!

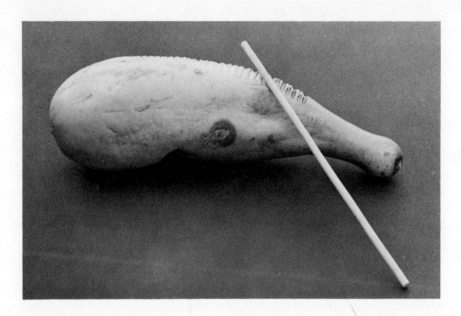

MATERIALS

1 large long dry gourd
Knife
Pencil
Triangular file
1 dowel or stick, ¼" in diameter and 12" long

TO MAKE

1. With a knife cut a 3" x 3" hole in the concave side of the gourd (A). This is the sound hole.

2. Scoop out all the membrane and seeds from the gourd. Dry gourd thoroughly—see Methods and Materials section for how to do this.
3. With a pencil mark ⅓" intervals on the opposite side from the sound hole (B).
4. With the file, make notches in the gourd, making sure not to file through the shell.

TO PLAY

Hold round, full end of gourd against upper arm. Rub rhythmically with the dowel.

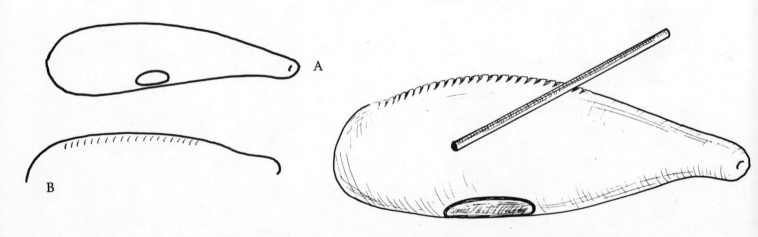

Nail Rasp

This makes a soft, bell-like sound.

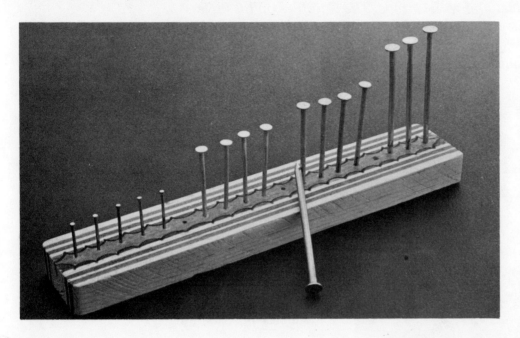

MATERIALS

1 block of wood 10″ x 2″ x 2″. Try to have the grain of the wood going across rather than lengthwise (this keeps the wood from splitting when hammering nails).
Nails of different sizes (16 were used in our diagram)
1 large nail for strumming
Hammer
Paint or marking pens (optional)

TO MAKE

1. Draw a line the length of the wood in the center (A).

2. Mark where to place nails (B). The nails are grouped according to sizes (C).
3. Hammer the nails in the marked spots.
4. If desired, the block of wood may be decorated with paint or marking pens.

TO PLAY

Use the large nail to run down the line of nails in a rhythmic fashion. The different lengths of the nails make different bell-like sounds.

C

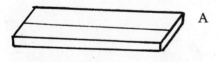

A

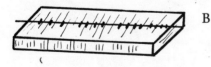

B

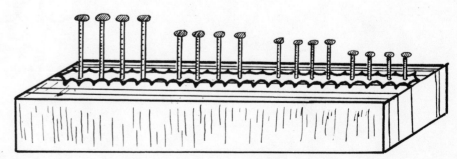

Washboard Rasp

One popular musician in Los Angeles anchors his large washboard to his chest with shoulder and waist straps. The thimbles on his fingers stroke and thump the metal, the wood, and the attached brass bells. The climax of his performance comes with the jangle of the attached tricycle bell and a raucous blare on a horn.

MATERIALS

1 washboard—any size will do
Paint (optional)
3 wooden spools from thread, small for small washboard or large for large washboard (A)
2 small wooden beads (B)
3 wooden cabinet knobs (C)
2 cabinet knobs to fit tops of spools (D)
1 nail for threading bead/spool/bead/knob
White glue
Tricycle bell, with screws for attaching (E)
Bicycle horn, with screws for attaching (F)
Thimbles for strumming

TO MAKE

1. Paint the washboard, if desired. Be sure not to paint the metal portion.
2. Attach the spools and knobs in any positions you would like (or use our diagram as a guide), by gluing them in place on the top of

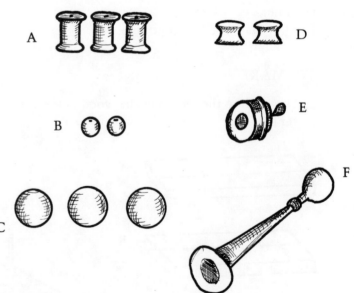

the washboard. Make sure that the glue dries thoroughly before you try to play the instrument. (We attached the center bead/spool/bead/knob by threading them on a nail about 4″ long, which we hammered in place.)

3. Attach the bell and the horn.

TO PLAY

Cover the fingers with thimbles, and rub and tap the metal ridges and the wooden frame. The board may be harnessed to the player's shoulders, as mentioned above, or it may be laid on his lap. One Chicago performer balances his on his lap and also thumps on a cow bell and a hollow block which are fastened to the frame. A talented performer at the National Folk Festival in Wolf Trap, Virginia, in the summer of 1976, had only the metal ridges, worn like a giant bib.

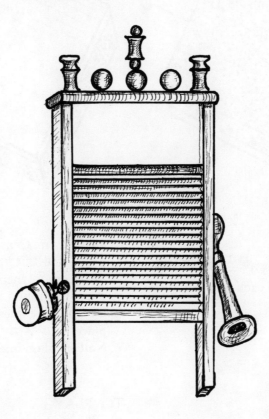

Sand Blocks

The sound produced by rubbing two sand blocks together may represent a soft summer breeze or the chug of a train, depending on the grade of sandpaper used.

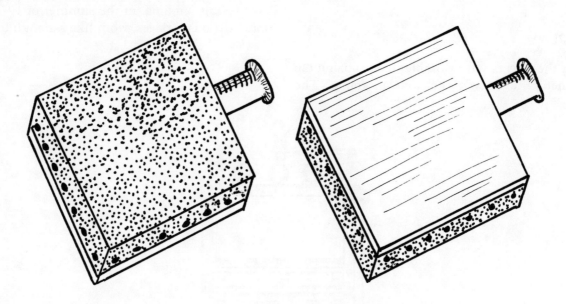

MATERIALS

2 wooden squares, each 5" x 5" x 1"
Sandpaper, to cover one side of each block
Spools, for handles (optional)
Tacks, glue or staples
Saw, scissors, hammer

TO MAKE

1. Cut the squares of wood to 5" x 5".
2. Cut the sandpaper to 6" x 6"; this will cover one side of each block and go ½" up each side.
3. Place sandpaper on flat surface with rough side down. Center wooden block over sandpaper and cut the corners out to achieve a neat corner, then bend the edges of the sandpaper up around the block (A).
4. Use tacks, staples or glue to hold sandpaper in place.
5. Nail spool on one edge of block for handle.

TO PLAY

Rub blocks together gently for a soft whispering accompaniment, or forcefully for the sound of marching feet or the puffing of a train.

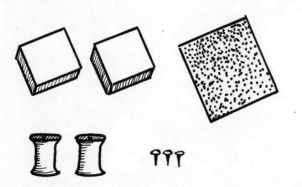

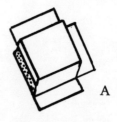

A

Pak'Papa (California Indian Clapper)

The peaceful Maidu and Miwak Indians of central California used this ingenious clapper instead of a heavy drum. The versatile elderberry bush provides fruit, wine and instruments.

MATERIALS

1 straight elderberry branch, 1½' to 2' long
Knife

TO MAKE

1. Cut branch while green and dry thoroughly.
2. With the knife, split the branch lengthwise along ¾ of its length.

3. Remove the pithy center with the knife, leaving the center hollow. Elderberry wood is tough but it will split occasionally. You will need patience, gentleness, and a long summer afternoon in the shade.

TO PLAY

Play rhythmically by shaking in right hand or by striking against the palm of the left hand.

Miwak Indian Ceremonial near Sutterville, California, 1974. PHOTOGRAPHED BY MICHAEL DUNNE.

Hawaiian Pu-Ilis

This was traditionally made by cutting long slits in the end of a heavy bamboo stalk. See References for information on the traditional music and dance.

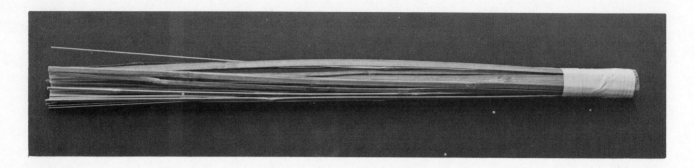

MATERIALS

Bamboo stick, approximately 25″ long and at least 1½″ in diameter, or an old bamboo porch shade

One 1″ dowel, 4″ long, for use with the bamboo porch shade

Fabric tape, for use with the bamboo porch shade

Knife

TO MAKE

1. For the bamboo stick: With a pocketknife, cut down the length of the stalk to 4″ from the end several times, making slits about every ⅓″. This will give you a fringed end (A).

2. For the bamboo porch shade: Remove string holding shade together. Cut to a 25″ length enough slats to completely encircle 1″ dowel. Wrap the slats around the dowel (B). Hold in place by wrapping handle with fabric tape.

TO PLAY

This instrument works best when several are played at the same time. The musicians sit in a row on the floor, and tap the bundles lightly on their arms and shoulders or their neighbors' backs, producing a soft rattling sound.

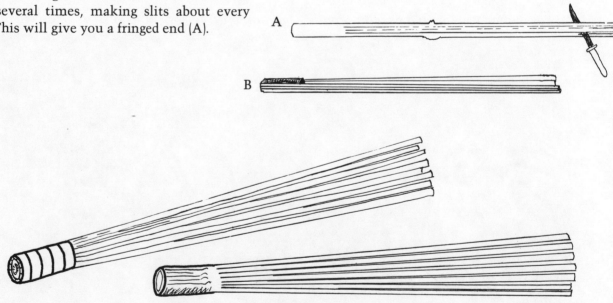

Philippine Tinakling Poles

Legend says that these giant rhythm sticks and the dancers that move around them are artistic representations of the Philippine lake shore where the long-legged crane wades through windblown reeds.

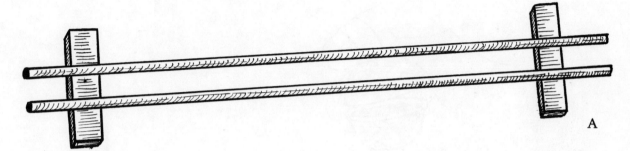

A

MATERIALS

2 bamboo poles, each 1" x 8' to 10' long (bamboo fishing poles would work nicely), or 2 wooden poles of the same size
2 wooden boards, each 1" x 25" x 2"
Saw

TO MAKE

1. Cut the two 1"-diameter poles to 8' to 10' long.
2. Cut the 1" base boards to 2" x 25". The lumber company will do this for you, or may have the sizes already in stock.

TO PLAY

Set the poles parallel, resting on the wooden base (A). One player sits at each end, one hand on each long pole. With synchronized motions they move the poles in three-quarter time:

Beat 1—Tap board with poles *apart* (B).
Beat 2—Tap board again with poles *apart* (C).
Beat 3—Tap poles *together* (D).

The dancer steps in and out of center space while moving to the rhythm of the tapping and singing. Reverse feet on each measure.

See References for further suggestions and music.

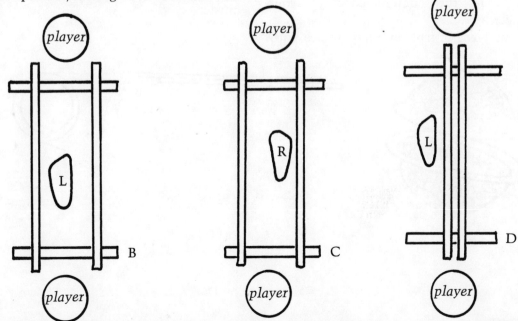

Walnut Castanets

Memories of nights in Mexico and Madrid . . .

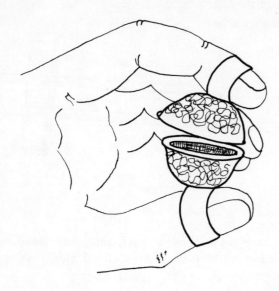

MATERIALS

2 walnut shell halves
Fabric tape
White glue
Nutcracker, scissors

TO MAKE

1. Crack the walnuts so the shell halves remain intact. Scrape out the membrane and walnut meat (A).
2. Cut 4 pieces of tape, two 1" longer than the circumference of your thumb and two 1" longer than the circumference of your forefinger.
3. Place one piece of tape on a flat surface with the adhesive side up. Place the adhesive side of other tape measuring the same length over the adhesive tape on the flat surface, allowing ½" at one end (B). This will allow the 2 pieces to adhere to each other when a ring is made (C). Repeat with second pair of tapes.
4. Place glue on fabric rings and attach firmly to the tops of the shell halves. Pressure often helps at this point. Dry thoroughly.

TO PLAY

Place the castanets on the thumb and forefinger and tap the two halves together to the beat of the music.

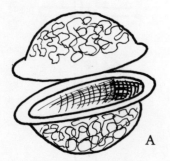

Bone Castanets

The "Mr. Bones" of the old minstrel show had great skill in using these rib bones as castanets. Recently a Southern politician played metal spoons in this same way to liven up his campaign trail.

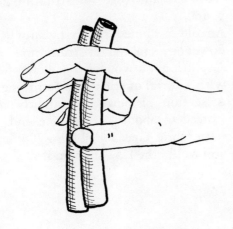

MATERIALS

2 slightly curved rib bones from pork spareribs, about 8" long, or bones from short ribs of beef
Soap
Scouring pad
Wax (optional; any paste wax will give a nice smooth finish)

TO MAKE

1. After a dinner of spareribs, select two bones of similar size.
2. Scrub bones clean with soap and a rough scouring pad.
3. Dry thoroughly.
4. Wax if desired.

TO PLAY

Hold loosely between fingers in one hand (see diagram), and shake or rattle like castanets, using the thumb at times.

Quick and Simple

Just as the title suggests, to make rhythm quickly.

1. Vegetable grater, with a thimble for strumming (A).
2. Two wooden spoons (B), played as you would the rhythm sticks, or in one hand like the bone castanets.
3. Two metal spoons (C), played Appalachian style like the bone castanets.
4. A section of a corrugated cardboard carton and a pencil or small stick. Remove the top layer of the cardboard (D)—this leaves you with a ripple edge for strumming with the pencil.
5. An old-fashioned steam radiator (E), with a dowel or metal rod for strumming.
6. A portion of wooden or metal fencing (F), with a dowel or stick for strumming.
7. A section of newspaper tightly rolled and fringed to about 3″ from one end. Tape end with fabric tape, for holding (G), and play as you would the Hawaiian pu-ilis.

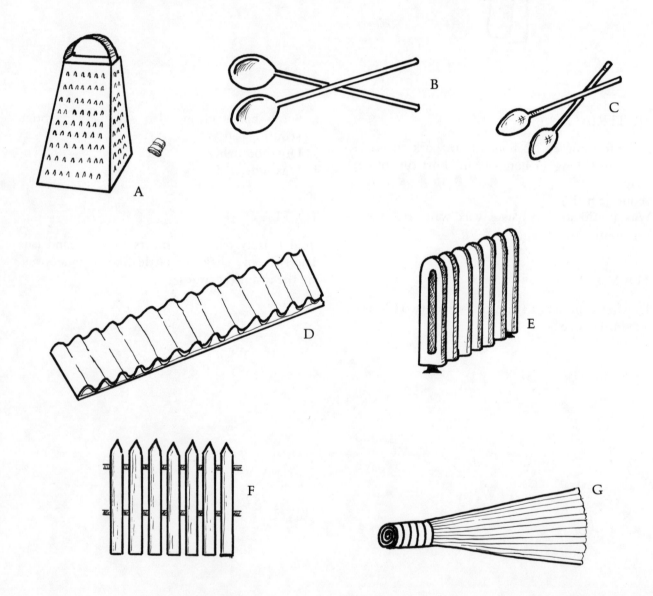

Jingle Bells
and
Rattles

History

While jingle bells and rattles are easy to make, there are many ways they can be played. The same simple shaker that an infant grasps as his or her first toy can also convey the complex rhythms of the skilled adult musician.

Rattles provide the background of many ceremonies. A birchbark rattle accompanies the mournful chant of a Northwest Indian funeral; a feathered gourd rattle accents the sensuous movements of a Hawaiian hula; the elegant Turkish crescent proclaimed the power of the ruler in seventeenth-century Europe.

Many different materials can be used for making jingle bells or rattles. Inhabitants of tropical climates use gourds and bamboo. Others may use seashells, seedpods, or rocks. Turtle shells and baskets are used by the Hopi Indians and the Congo Ubangi. Where metal is available it is used for bells. The nineteenth-century American Indians prized the empty metal spice boxes of the settlers. Tin cans were cut into small cylinders and even empty metal cartridges were used.

Bright paint, ribbons and colored beads are additions which give visual excitement to the instruments. These accessories enhance the satisfaction gained from the performance by both the listener and the performer.

Gourd Rattle

Gourds are easy to grow. They can often be found in the market, especially in a local farmers' market. The type and amount of rattles used inside change the sound dramatically.

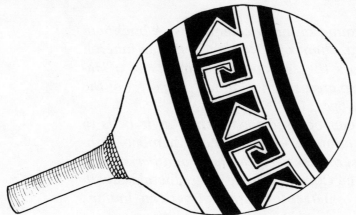

MATERIALS

1 dried gourd, any shape or size, but hard and firm

Rattles—seeds from gourd, pebbles, beans

Knife or hand saw, to cut neck of gourd

Narrow spoon or knife

Dowel or stick, 6″ long and the width of neck of gourd in diameter, if necessary

Twine or heavy string

White glue

Poster paints and shellac (optional)

TO MAKE

1. With knife, cut off the narrow end of the gourd; if neck is long enough, leave most on for handle (A).
2. With narrow spoon or knife, scoop out seeds and membrane inside the gourd. Save seeds for rattle.
3. Dry gourd in the hot sun or oven at a low even temperature (see Methods and Materials section).
4. When dry, fill gourd with seeds, beans or pebbles.
5. If it's long enough for a handle, reattach gourd end with white glue.
6. If dowel is needed for handle, place glue on one end of dowel and insert in the neck of gourd (B). Dry. Dip twine in white glue and wrap firmly around dowel and up the gourd about ½″ (C).
7. If desired, paint a bright colorful design on gourd with poster paint; when dry, shellac to protect finish. Or you may leave it natural.

TO PLAY

Shake rhythmically.

HINTS

A long season of drying in the warm sun and wind is the best for gourds. In colder climates the process can be speeded by a warm oven. Be sure the gourd is completely dry before cutting, otherwise it will shrink and wrinkle.

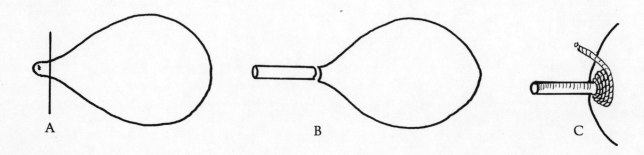

A   B   C

Hawaiian Uli-Uli

This is the Hawaiian version of the gourd rattle. The hula dancer carries it with the gourds downward to emphasize the movement of the bright feathers and the movement of her grass skirt.

MATERIALS

2 dried gourds, each about 3″ in diameter

Spoon or knife, for cutting and scooping out gourd

2 dowels, each about 5″ long and wide enough in diameter to fit neck of gourd

Beans, for rattles

White glue

¼″ plywood, 5″ x 10″, to make two 5″ circles

Saw, hand or electric

2 nails

Hammer

Feathers or crepe paper—enough to decorate the plywood discs

TO MAKE

1. With a knife, cut off the neck end of each of the gourds, leaving enough of the neck to insert a dowel for a handle (A).

2. Scoop out seeds and membrane with a spoon or knife.

3. Dry gourd in the hot sun or oven at a low even temperature (see Methods and Materials section).

4. Cut two 5″ circles from the plywood (B). Center a nail in each circle and nail through to dowels (C).

5. Insert about 10 beans for rattles in gourds. Place glue on dowel, insert in neck of gourd and dry (D).

6. Attach feathers or crepe paper to plywood circles with glue or staples.

TO PLAY

The dancers hold a shaker in each hand, with the gourd down and the feathers up to accent the traditional hand movements of the hula. At intervals, they tap the gourd half of one instrument on the feathered wood circle of the other.

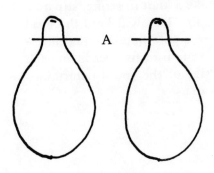

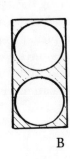

A

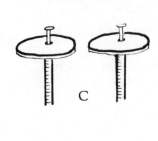

B

C

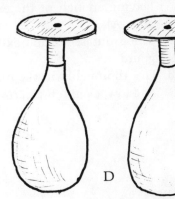

D

Calabash

Originally from Africa, but now common in Latin America, this large calabash has its rattles outside. The most effective sound comes when there are many small glass beads on a loose network of strings.

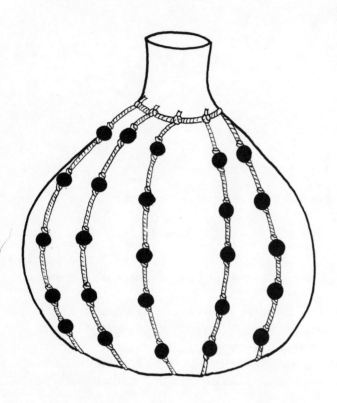

MATERIALS

Gourd, preferably about 6" in diameter with a neck as pictured
String or cord, thin enough to slip through beads
Beads, wooden or glass
Candle wax
Masking or cellophane tape
Scissors

TO MAKE

1. With a knife, cut off narrow end of the gourd, leaving enough of the end to grasp comfortably (A).
2. Scoop out seeds and extra membrane in the gourd.
3. Dry thoroughly in the hot sun or in the oven at a low, even temperature.
4. Cut a piece of string about 4" long and tie it in a circle (B). Lay on a flat surface.
5. Cut 12 pieces of string (more for a larger gourd), each about twice the height of the gourd, or at least long enough to tie knots on each side of each bead and to knot at base of gourd. Tie these strings at equal intervals around the circle of string (C).
6. Dip free end of each string in melted candle wax, to make threading beads easier. When burning a candle, enough wax forms around the candle wick to dip string. Let wax on string harden. Make a knot in string, slip on a bead and knot again. This will hold the bead in place. Repeat this procedure at equal intervals until you have four or five beads on each string (D). The size of the gourd determines how many beads to use.

7. Tape circle with beads onto the rounded top of gourd; use masking tape or cellophane tape (E).
8. Loosely tie a circle of string around the handle base (F). This will hold the beaded strings in place.
9. Attach the beaded strings with knots to the string circle, adjusting them so that the strings are loose and will rattle against the side of the gourd.

TO PLAY

This is especially fun to play because, besides just being shaken, it can be tossed and caught—in rhythm, of course.

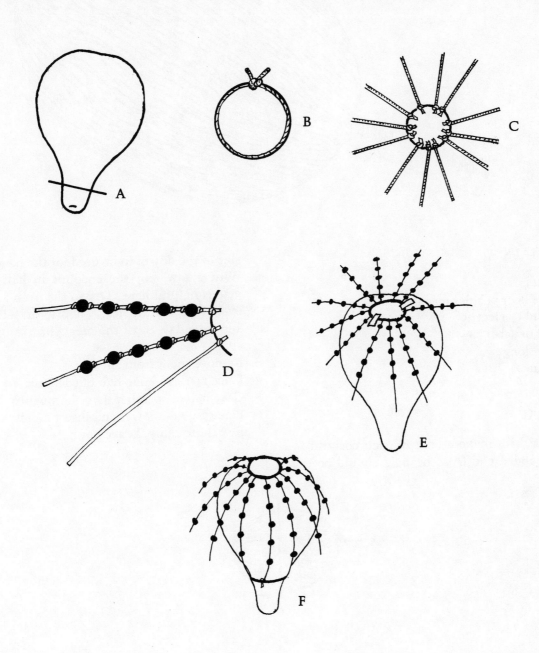

Coconut Rattle

This is an almost unbreakable instrument, but it is a challenge to saw and drill.

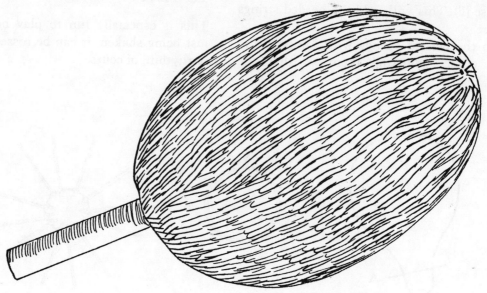

MATERIALS

2 coconuts
Beads, seeds or pebbles for rattles
Drill, hand or electric
Hacksaw or saber saw
Dowel, 5" long
White glue

TO MAKE

1. With a drill, make a hole in each coconut at the rounded end (A). The hole should be the size of the dowel to be used for the handle.
2. With a saw, cut the coconut in half (B). (A vise is helpful here.) Dry in the oven at a low, even temperature for 2 hours, or set in the sun for a day, until the meat shrinks from the shell.
3. Remove meat from shell.
4. Place rattles in one half of coconut.
5. Glue halves together. Dry thoroughly.
6. Place glue on dowel and insert handle in hole. Dry thoroughly. Leave natural.

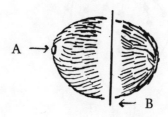

Metal Can Rattle

Some cultures have coconuts and bamboo to use for instruments; we can recycle our tin cans.

MATERIALS

Juice or soft drink can, metal or cardboard
Knife (for cardboard) or tinsnips (for metal)
Rice, macaroni or beans for rattles
Fabric tape
Construction paper
White glue
Marking pens
5" dowel for handle (optional)
Nail and hammer, if using dowel

TO MAKE

1. Cut the can ½" from the bottom, using a knife if cardboard, tinsnips if metal (A).

2. Mark center of bottom of can. Place dowel on underside of can at center. Nail through center of can to dowel to make handle (B).
3. Place rattles in container. Tape cut edges back together (C).
4. Tape soda can over opening (D); tape juice can around top edge (E).
5. Wrap construction paper around can and glue in place. Decorate with marking pens.

HINT

A set of small juice cans without handles with different rattles (pebbles, marbles, etc.) makes a truly "educational" toy for a small child.

A

B

C

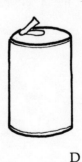
D

E

Balloon Rattle

Make your own gourd if you can't grow one!

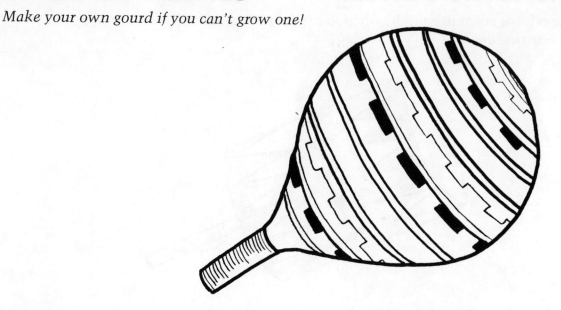

MATERIALS

Inexpensive balloon
Newspaper
White glue or flour and water, or wallpaper paste
½"-diameter dowel, 4" long
Popcorn, beans or small pebbles for rattles

TO MAKE

1. Inflate balloon and tie end.
2. Tear (do not cut) newspaper into 2" squares.
3. If using white glue, dilute with an equal amount of water in a container. If flour and water is used, make a paste, making sure it is not too runny. For wallpaper paste, follow directions on package.
4. Dip newspaper in paste and cover balloon with several (about 4) layers, making sure the paper extends down around tied end of balloon so that the dowel handle can be inserted later (A).
5. Hang overnight in a warm place to dry thoroughly.
6. Prick balloon and remove it from the dried papier mâché form.
7. Insert about ¼ cup of rattles (popcorn, or beans, etc.) through hole.
8. Glue dowel handle in opening of balloon.
9. Decorate with marking pens or poster paint.

HINT

An even temperature while drying will insure that the form will retain its round shape.

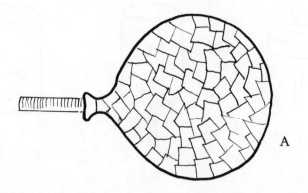

A

Light Bulb Rattle

Preschoolers can make this with proper precautions. Just be sure the coating is thick and heavy so the glass can't escape.

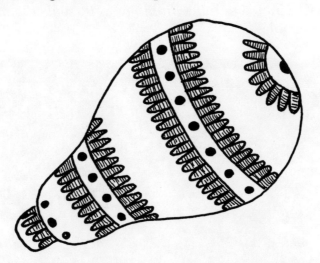

MATERIALS

1 large light bulb, 100 watts or more
Newspaper
White glue, flour-and-water paste, or wallpaper
   paste
Poster paint or marking pens
Plastic spray

TO MAKE

1. Tear (do not cut) newspaper into 1″ squares.
2. Make a paste of equal parts of water and white glue; or make a flour and water paste that is not too runny; or prepare wallpaper paste (directions on package).
3. Dip newspaper squares into paste mixture and cover light bulb completely. Add newspaper until there is a heavy coat—at least 6 layers—completely covering the bulb and its base (A).
4. Dry thoroughly.
5. Break covered bulb: Hit lightly on countertop or with a hammer until glass jingles. The glass inside gives the very nice rattle sound.
6. Decorate with poster paint or marking pens and spray with a clear plastic to preserve the finish.

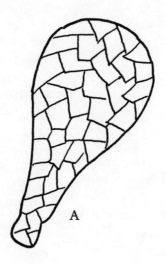

A

Navajo Drum Rattle

This special drumstick rattle, used by the Navajo Indians, allows the musician to play two instruments at the same time. This is an easy version of the original, which was made from rawhide, soaked and dried around sand or pebbles.

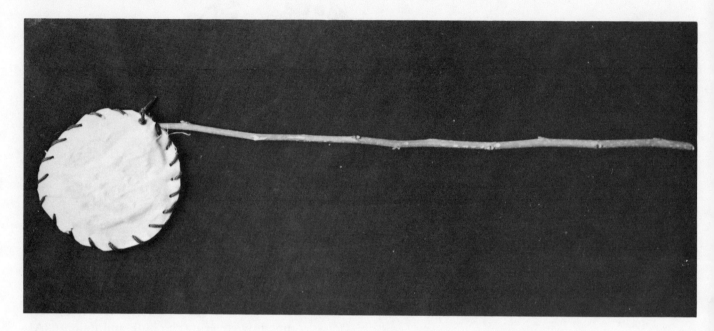

MATERIALS

Fresh thin branch, about 15″ long, strong and
   limber
Wrapping twine
6″ x 12″ piece of lightweight cotton fabric
White glue
2 small fruit bowls
Wax paper
Beans for rattles
Shoestring, at least 36″ long
Paper punch or fabric punch

TO MAKE

1. Bend one end of branch, making a loop about
   4″ in diameter. Tie with twine to hold in
   place (A). Soak or whittle if necessary to obtain a circular shape.
2. Cut fabric in a circle and about 2″ larger than
   loop in branch.

3. Wet fabric thoroughly in a solution of 3 parts
   white glue and 1 part water. Place wax paper
   over small fruit bowls, and lay wet fabric over
   bowls (B). The fabric will dry hard and retain
   the bowl shape.
4. Dry thoroughly.
5. Place one piece of fabric on each side of loop
   in branch. Trim all around to ½″ from branch.
   With punch, make holes every ½″ around circle (C).
6. Using shoestring, lace fabric around branch.
   When about halfway around, place about 10
   beans inside fabric; finish the lacing and tie.

TO PLAY

By hitting the fabric end of the rattle on a
drum, you make rattle and drum noises
simultaneously.

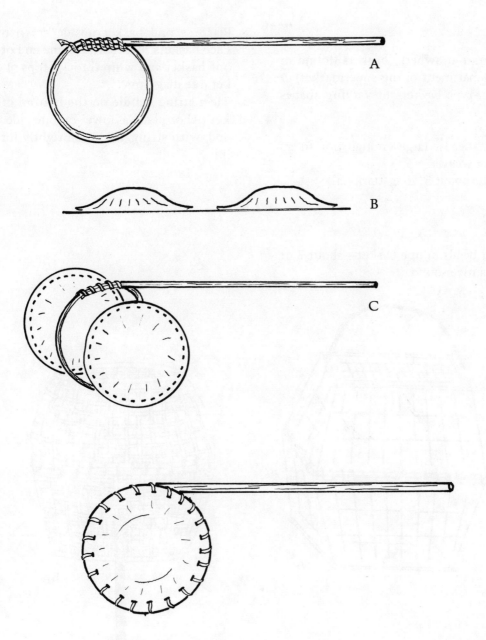

Basket Rattle

Found worldwide from Africa through the Pacific Islands to the American Southwest. The beads or bells are especially important, since the basket material provides little sound.

MATERIALS

2 plastic tomato or strawberry baskets (found in the produce department of the supermarket) or 2 small Easter-type baskets of varying shapes and sizes

String

Bells or wooden beads, large enough not to go through basket weave

Dowel for handle, about 5″ long (optional)

TO MAKE

1. Place bells or beads in one basket—about 7 or 8 will make a nice sound.

2. Place second basket upside down over first. Lace baskets together: Tie one end of string to one basket and whip through tops of each basket (see diagrams).

3. Tie a string handle on the bottom of one basket (A) or place a dowel on one side of basket and, with string, lace it on tightly for a handle (B).

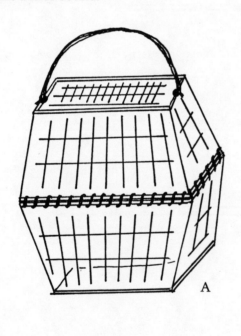

A

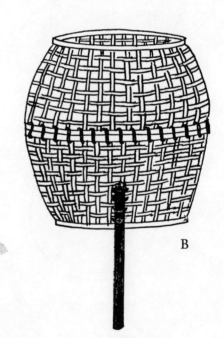

B

Indian Dancing Bells

Dancers often use bells for decoration and sound. The American Indians used them everywhere—neck, waist, wrist, knee or ankle. Colored feathers accent the bells.

MATERIALS

3 to 5 bells (Christmas bells or small bells from import or hobby shops)
Leather strip, 2" x 6"
Leather lacing or shoestring
Scissors or mat knife

TO MAKE

1. Make slits in leather with scissors or mat knife—one at each end and the rest in groups of two (A).
2. With one continuous piece of leather lacing, string bells onto leather strip, leaving enough at each end for tying around arm or leg.
3. Decorate leather strip with feathers by gluing feathers under bells.

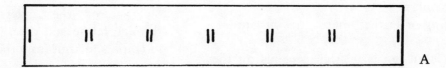

A

Apache Dancing Bells

*This idea was common among many Indian tribes. Our sample comes
from the White Mountain Apache tribe. Originally shells or animal
teeth were probably used, but the tin cones used in the last century
make a more exciting sound.*

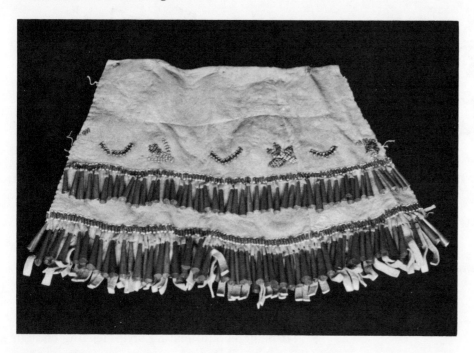

MATERIALS

Tin from tin cans

Tinsnips

Needlenose pliers

Leather lacing or leather shoestring, cut into 4"
  strips

Leather or fabric for base (this depends on the
  item on which you wish to use the bells)

Iron-on tape

TO MAKE

1. With the tinsnips, cut a "truncated triangle"
   shape from a flattened tin can as shown in
   Diagram A. Take care not to cut yourself on
   the tin.
2. Tie a knot in one end of 4" leather string.
   Center lacing on piece of tin (B).
3. With needlenose pliers bend tin piece around
   leather lacing, leaving enough lacing at the
   top to knot to leather or fabric (C).
4. To attach lacing to fabric, reinforce with iron-
   on tape on the underside; make a hole
   through fabric and tape. Insert leather lacing
   in fabric and knot from the back.

HINTS

These bells can be made into necklaces by tying
bells to a 1" x 12" piece of leather or fabric (D).
They may also be attached to the hem of a skirt
(E) or the sides of pants (F). If you wish to add
more decoration, this can be done with beads,
fabric tape, or embroidery.

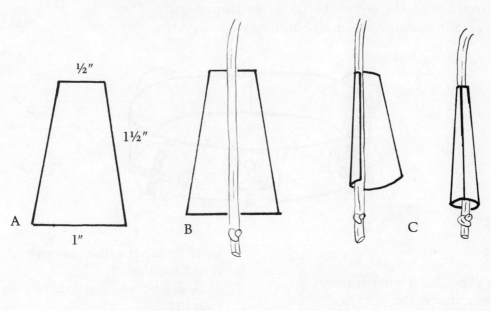

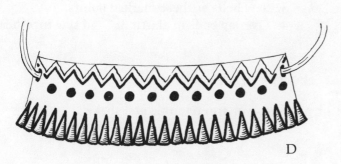

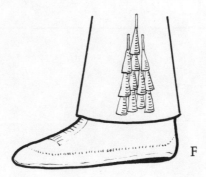

Elastic Dancing Bells

The modern touch of elastic allows better fit for arm or ankle. This version is especially suitable for small children who can't tie.

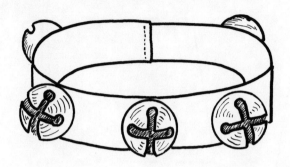

MATERIALS

½"- to 1"-wide elastic to fit wrist or ankle
5 to 7 bells, any size or shape
Large needle
Heavy-duty thread
Scissors

TO MAKE

1. Cut elastic to the size desired for ankle or wrist. Be sure to allow an extra ½" for sewing elastic together.
2. Mark elastic at equal intervals for attaching bells (A).
3. Sew bells at these marked points.
4. Overlap ends of elastic ½" and sew together.

TO PLAY

Slip over arm or ankle and shake.

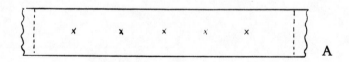

A

Jewelry Rattles

Any material will do. Whether you live by the ocean or inland, you can find materials that can be strung for decoration and musical effect.

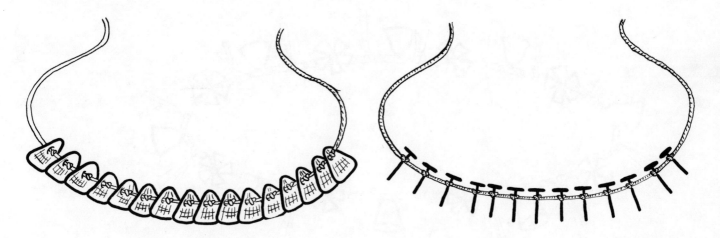

MATERIALS

About 20 of any of the following: seedpods, nut-shells, seashells, flat stones with holes, reso-nant hardwood sticks, hollow bamboo, small nails, with heads

Twine or leather shoestring about 36″ long

Drill

TO MAKE

1. Drill a hole the size of the twine or shoestring in the top edge of pods, shells, hardwood or bamboo (A).

2. Tie a knot in string, and string a shell (pod, wood, etc.); tie another knot to hold in place and repeat this procedure until the desired number of pieces are on the necklace (B). For nails, tie string securely under the head of each nail (C). Be sure not to tie the pieces too far apart because the pieces hitting together gives off the nice gentle sound.

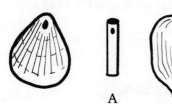

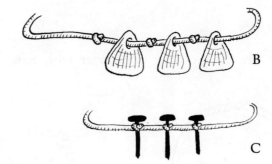

Flower Wreath and Bells

A natural accessory for girls' dancing groups. The hoop can be held in the hand, worn as a crown, or slipped around the neck according to the mood of the dancer and the style of the dance.

MATERIALS

1 wire coathanger
Wire cutters
Pliers
Floral tape or fabric tape
Lightweight floral wire
8 paper flowers; these can be made out of colored tissue or crepe paper
8 bells
Sixteen 12" pieces of ribbon or yarn

TO MAKE

1. Cut the hook off the coathanger with wire cutters. Bend the wire around a large jar or bucket to obtain a circle of the desired size. Twist wire ends tightly together with pliers to secure (A).
2. Attach bells at equal intervals; insert floral or fabric tape through hole in bell and twist over wire (B).
3. Make a flower by cutting three 2" x 4" strips of tissue or crepe paper. With floral wire, twist center of these into a tight knot. Secure floral wire to wreath with floral tape (C). Place paper flowers at equal intervals around wreath.
4. Attach pieces of ribbon or yarn between bells and flowers with a lark's-head knot (D).

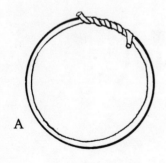

Tin Pan Tambourine

An easy substitute for a tambourine.

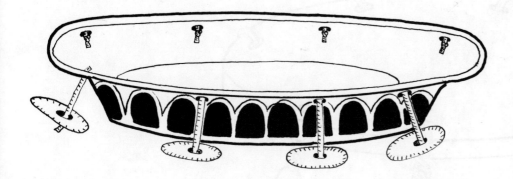

MATERIALS

1 metal pie tin, any size
Model paint or acrylic paint (optional)
8 metal bottle caps
Twine or heavy cord
Pliers
Hammer
Ice pick or punch

TO MAKE

1. Decorate the metal pie tin if desired, by using model paint or an acrylic paint.
2. With a punch or ice pick, punch holes at equal intervals around the edge of the pie tin (A).
3. With pliers, bend the edges of the bottle caps outward, then flatten with a hammer on a hard surface.
4. To remove cork or plastic, pliers are used to hold cap. Place over heat on stove to melt plastic (use good ventilation). Cork can usually be scraped off. Adults should help children!
5. With the punch, make a hole in the center of each of the flattened bottle caps (B).
6. Cut a 5″ piece of twine or cord. Tie a knot at one end; slip on bottle cap (C). Slip string through hole in pie tin and knot. Repeat until all caps are in place on tin.

TO PLAY

Shake. The caps hitting the pie tin make a nice jingling sound.

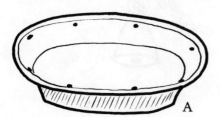

A

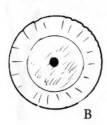

B

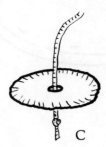

C

Plastic Tambourine

Some preschools use these by the dozen. They are easy to hold and they are unbreakable!

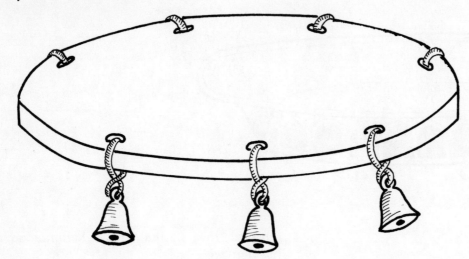

MATERIALS

1 plastic lid, at least 5″ in diameter—for example,
   the lid from a 2-pound coffee can
3 or 4 pipecleaners
5 to 7 inexpensive bells
Scissors

TO MAKE

1. With scissors, punch holes at equal intervals
   around the edge of plastic lid (A).
2. Cut the pipecleaners in half, and attach one
   piece to each bell by twisting (B).
3. Place one end of each piece of pipecleaner
   through hole in top of lid; twist together with
   other end to hold securely (C).

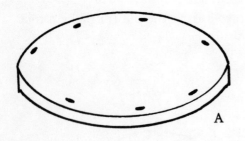

A

B

C

Handle Bells

The quality and number of bells used makes a difference.

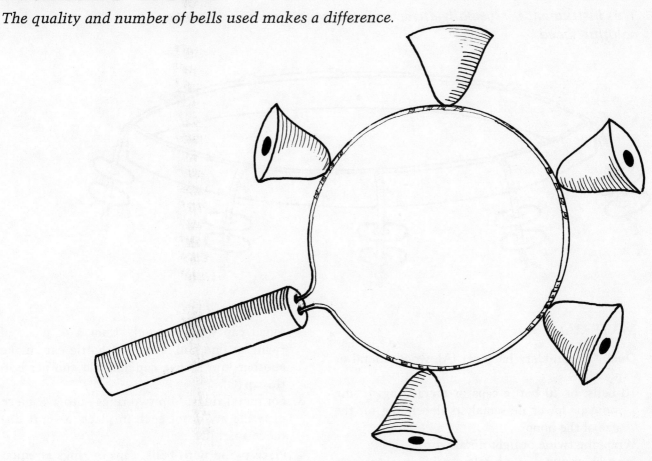

MATERIALS

5″ dowel, at least ¾″ in diameter
Wire coathanger
1 pint jar, approximately 3″ in diameter
5 bells
Floral or fabric tape
Wire cutters
Drill (hand or electric), with bit the diameter of
   coathanger wire
White glue

TO MAKE

1. With drill, drill two holes in the end of dowel handle to hold coathanger wire (A).
2. With wire cutters, cut the hook of the coathanger off; wrap the remaining wire around a pint jar, leaving ¾″ at each end to insert in dowel. Cut off excess wire (B). (One hanger has enough wire for three bells.)
3. Place glue in hole in dowel, and force wire stems into the glued hole. Dry thoroughly.
4. Attach bells at equal intervals around the circular wire with floral tape.

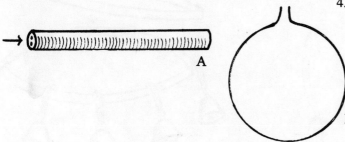

A

B

Circle Bells

This instrument is especially attractive with good quality bells and a colorful "head."

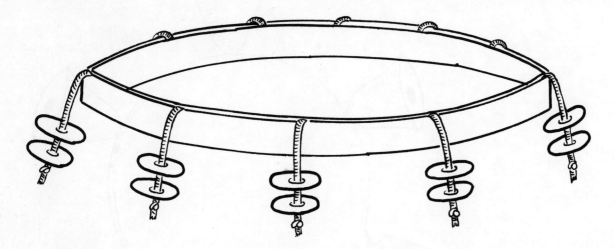

MATERIALS

One 5″ embroidery hoop set (A), wood, metal or plastic

10 bells, or 20 bottle caps or metal rings (using more or fewer noisemakers depending on the size of the hoop)

Wrapping twine or light floral wire

Ice pick or punch (for bottle caps)

Scissors or wire cutters

TO MAKE

1. For bells: Center each bell on a 4″ piece of twine; knot in place (B).
2. For bottle caps: With pliers, bend edges outward. Flatten caps with a hammer on a hard surface. Make a hole in the center of each flattened cap with ice pick. Knot a 4″ piece of twine at one end, slip on a bottle cap, make another knot above cap and add another bottle cap (C).
3. For metal rings: Slip two rings onto a 4″ piece of twine and knot each in place, a short distance apart (D).
4. Place twine with bells, caps or rings at equal intervals around outer embroidery hoop.
5. Place glue on the inside rim of the outer hoop and slip over the inner hoop (E).

HINTS

This can also be a tambourine. Use a round piece of leather, tire tubing or cloth (dipped in a solution of equal parts of white glue and water) as the head between the hoops.

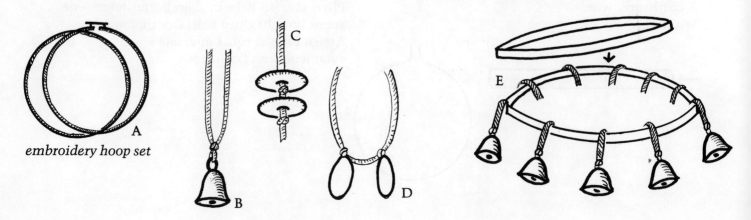

embroidery hoop set

Paper Plate Tambourine

An exciting project for children—in a short time they can create their own decorated instruments and dance with them.

MATERIALS

2 shallow paper bowls or 2 foil pie pans
Beans, rice or pebbles for rattles
White glue
Scissors
Yarn or ribbon for streamers
Marking pens (for paper plate)

TO MAKE

1. Decorate each paper bowl with marking pens in a colorful design. Foil pie tins don't have to be decorated—the silver and colorful streamers look exciting.
2. Place about ¼ cup of beans, rice or pebbles in one bowl (A).
3. Put glue on the edge of the bowl.
4. Place second bowl on top, pressing firmly until glue dries thoroughly—about 20 minutes (B).
5. With scissors, punch small holes at equal intervals around the edge, through both bowls (C).
6. Attach yarn or ribbon for streamers through holes.

HINT

Staples can be used to hold paper bowls or plates together.

Wooden Bottle-Cap Jingler

Constructing this instrument gives an extra psychological benefit—you get to pound the bottle caps.

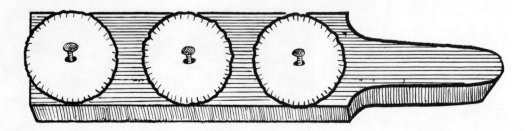

MATERIALS

1 block of wood, 8" x 1½" x ¾"
6 metal bottle caps
3 nails, each 1½" long
Hammer
Pliers
Ice pick or punch

TO MAKE

1. Cut a 2¾" handle at one end of the block of wood (A). This is optional but is nice for the finished piece.
2. With pliers, bend out edges of bottle caps, then flatten with a hammer on a hard surface. To remove cork, use pliers to hold cap. Place over heat on stove until cork is burned away. This is best done with adult help for small children.
3. With ice pick or punch, make a hole in the center of each bottle cap, making sure the hole is wider than the nail's shank but narrower than its head.
4. Place each nail through two caps (B). Position nails at equal intervals on wooden block, making sure the caps do not touch each other. Hammer nails in loosely so the caps will jingle.

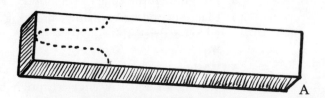

A

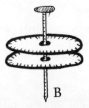

B

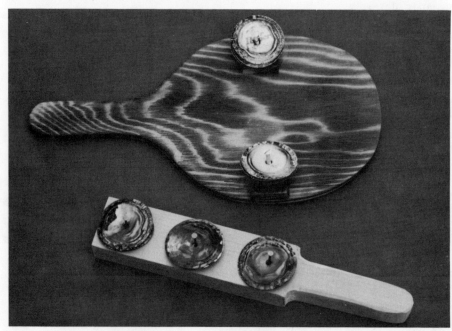

Wooden Paddle Jingler

A larger version of the previous shaker.

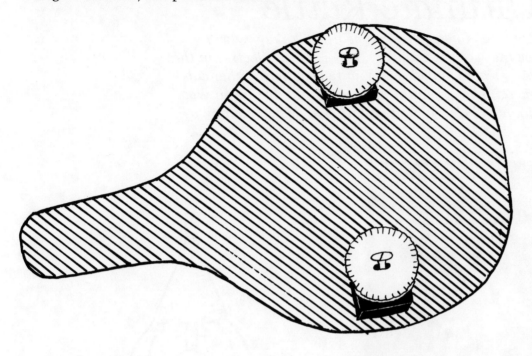

MATERIALS

1 piece of ¼" plywood—10" x 6"—or an old ping
  pong paddle
Coping saw or electric hand saw
2 small blocks of wood, each 2"x 1" x ½"
6 metal bottle caps
2 wood screws, each 1¼" long
Screwdriver
Hammer
White glue

TO MAKE

1. With saw, cut a paddle shape to fill the 10" x
   6" piece of ¼" plywood (A). A purchased paddle or old ping pong paddle will also work
   nicely.

2. Glue the small blocks of wood 2" down from
   top and ½" in from the sides (B).
3. With pliers, bend out edges of caps (this
   makes the flattening easier). Flatten caps with
   a hammer on a hard surface. To remove cork,
   hold cap with pliers over burner on stove until cork is burned away. Adults, please help
   children with this step.
4. With an ice pick or punch, make a hole in the
   center of each bottle cap. The hole should be
   larger than the shank of the screw.
5. Place three caps on each screw. Center screws
   on the small blocks and screw in place (C).
   Don't screw too tightly, for the caps must be
   loose to jingle.

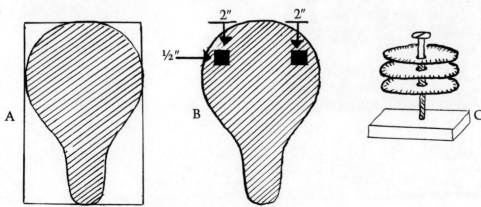

Turkish Crescent or Johnny Jingle —The Ultimate Rattle

This elaborate rattle came to western Europe from Turkey, where it had been used since the sixteenth century. It was most effective in the military bands which accompanied the mounted soldiers. Other cultures have used this same idea—in the southern United States it was called a "Jingling Johnny." Use your creativity and design your own version.

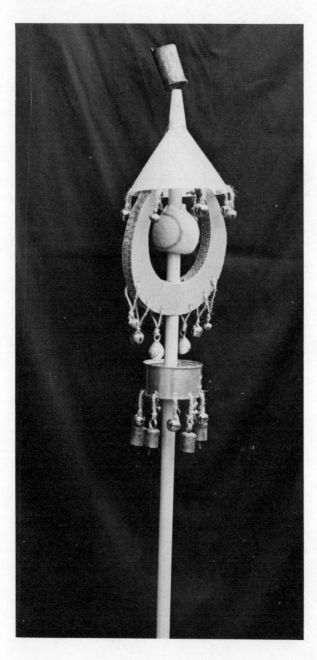

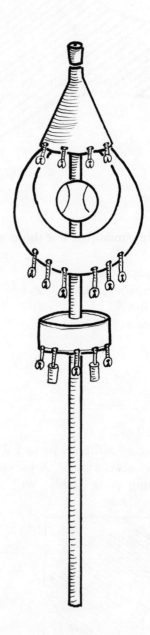

MATERIALS

1 dowel, ¾" x 36"
1 7-oz. tuna can, or a can of that size
28 bells of different sizes and shapes
1 elephant bell (optional)
8 nails, each about 1½" long
Wrapping twine
1 cardboard box, large enough to provide 4 pieces
  of cardboard, each 10" x 10"
1 old tennis ball, or a ball of that size
Funnel, plastic or metal, about 6" in diameter
Hammer
Tinsnips
Drill
Knife or saw for cardboard
Punch
Screwdriver
White glue
Paint

TO MAKE

1. Hammer four nails into dowel, 24" up from bottom, to hold tuna can in place (A).
2. In the center of the tuna can, punch a hole; enlarge with tinsnips. The hole should be large enough to slip over the dowel (B).
3. With punch or ice pick, punch 10 holes evenly spaced around opposite edge of can (C).
4. String 10 of the bells and tie around the edge of can (D).
5. Slip can over dowel so it sits over the nails. Hammer one more nail to each side of dowel, about ½" above the can (E).
6. Glue the 4 pieces of 10" x 10" cardboard together (F). Dry thoroughly.
7. Draw a horseshoe shape on the cardboard, making sure the open end of the horseshoe will just fit inside of the funnel (G). Cut out the horseshoe shape with a sharp knife or saw.
8. Make a hole down through the center of the cardboard horseshoe with a screwdriver, large enough to let the dowel slip through.
9. Slide cardboard horseshoe over dowel to about 3" above tuna can; nail or glue in place (H). At the base of horseshoe make 3 holes, evenly spaced, on each side of dowel, using a hammer and a large nail. Attach string to each of 6 bells and insert through holes. Knot the end of each string, being sure to allow enough length so bells will dangle (I).
10. Cut an X in the top and bottom of a tennis ball (J). Place 2 small bells in the ball. Slip

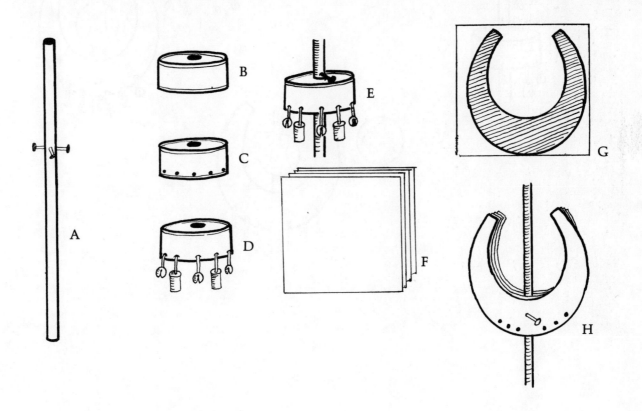

ball over dowel (K). The ball will stay in place if the X's are not too large.

11. With the drill, make 10 holes evenly spaced around the edge of the funnel. With twine tie the remaining 10 bells to funnel (L).

12. Place funnel over dowel, making sure that the funnel touches the top of the cardboard horseshoe. If it does not touch, saw the top off the dowel. Place glue on cardboard horseshoe and the top of the dowel and position funnel.

13. With a drill, make a hole through funnel and dowel. Insert nail (M). This will keep the funnel in place when the Johnny Jingle is thumped on the floor.

14. Nail the elephant bell upside down to the top of the dowel, just inside the tip of the funnel. This is optional.

15. Paint and add colored streamers to suit your imagination.

TO PLAY

The long handle is used to shake the bells as well as to pound on the floor if more sound is desired. In Chicago, Svoboda's Nickelodeon Tavern and Museum features a Zing-a-boom, an elaborate Johnny Jingle with a strong spring on the bottom of the handle. The performer pounds the thick post on the floor while he beats the small drum and cymbal which are attached to the top of the instrument. The result is drum, rattles, and jingles in a combination that is exciting to the eye as well as to the ear.

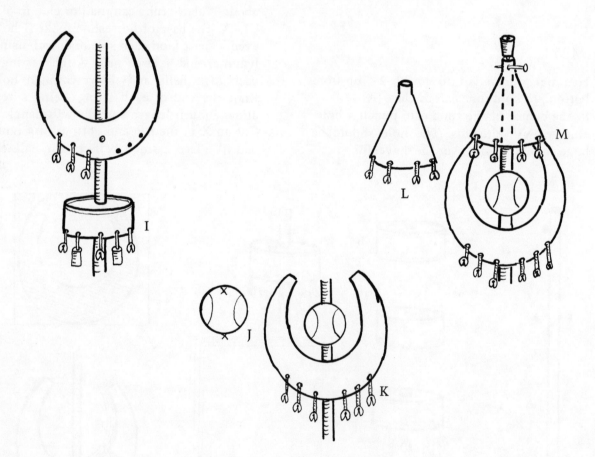

Quick and Simple

A sampling of easy ideas that can be produced on the spot, like instant coffee.

1. Cardboard roll rattle. Tape one end of cardboard roll (paper towel, etc.) closed. Place beans in roll for rattles. Tape open end. Decorate with marking pens (A).
2. Tennis ball can. This is an easy version of the African tubo. Usually made from a long tube of bamboo or metal, it is used by modern rock groups. Empty one small box of BB's into a tennis ball can with a plastic lid. Tape lid closed and shake (B).
3. Plastic fruit rattle. With scissors, enlarge holes in a plastic lemon or lime juice container. Place beans in container. Screw on top and shake (C).
4. Tea strainer rattle. Place beads in one tea strainer; place second strainer on top. Lace the two strainers together with string (D). Shake.
5. Plastic detergent container rattle. Wash and dry a container with a narrow neck. Place small nails in container, screw on top, and shake (E).
6. Paper bag rattle. Decorate a small paper bag with poster paints or marking pens. Place beans in bag and tie with bright colored yarn (F).
7. Balloon rattle. Place several beans in a small balloon for rattles. Blow up balloon and tie end (G). Shake.
8. Metal box rattle. Place beans in a small metal box (adhesive bandage or candy box). Tape lid closed with masking or fabric tape (H). Shake.

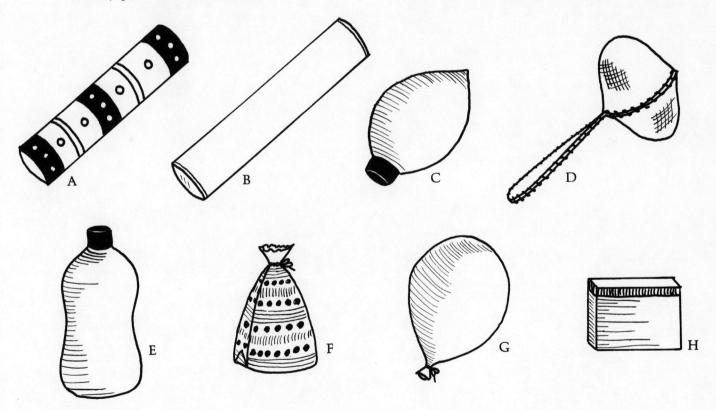

Gongs, Blocks and Xylophones

History

"Drumming on a hollow log" is a common phrase. Technically, however, a hollow log is not a drum. In a more highly developed form it is called a slit drum, but it is a solid vibrating object and belongs to a class of percussion instruments called idiophones. A true drum makes sound because of a taut vibrating membrane.

Solid objects which vibrate with a tonal quality may be made from many different materials and in many different sizes. In the New Hebrides Islands the primitive log instrument has been developed into a huge carved hollow wooden figure that is upended in a "drum grove" of other tuned logs. The famous African "telegraph drum," used to relay messages over a long distance, is a skillfully crafted slit drum. Heavy bamboo stalks provide a ready-made material for instruments of this type in tropical climates.

Rocks are used as idiophones in other parts of the world. On the Canadian shore of Lake Ontario are two tall granite rocks called "Bell Rocks." The Ojibway Indians say their forefathers sounded an alarm around the bay by striking these huge boulders with their war clubs. In China this type of sound was highly developed thousands of years ago. The Heavenly Temple at Peking has sixteen tuned slabs of green nephrite, and numerous marble stones are found in the monasteries. Confucius wrote that musical ceremonies should begin with a bell and end with a sonorous stone.

Xylophones made from tuned metal, wood and bamboo are found worldwide. Many have special sounding chambers made from gourds or coconuts. Some inventive modern musicians have made them from prehistoric bones and plate glass. *

The centuries-old African thumb piano has become popular recently. There are many versions—small and delicate for private songs (in small apartments) or large and tuned in the eight-tone Western scale to accompany any song. Modern microphones make it possible for the delicate vibrations from the metal tines to be heard in a large concert hall.

Immigrants to the Americas used their Old World musical ideas with New World materials. They suspended farm implements for chuckwagon gongs, they drummed frying pans as substitute African bells (metal bells with no clapper) and, in Trinidad, they even played harmony on leftover oil drums. You can hear these steel drum bands all over the United States. Central Park, in New York City, is full of them on summer evenings.

*See References: Weidemann, Music in Sticks and Stones.

Singing Rocks

A remarkable instrument put together and named by Mary Aspaas of Cornville, Arizona. She plays over 150 songs and has performed at many Gem and Mineral shows in the Southwest. The directions for making are quoted here in her own words.

MATERIALS

Phonolite, a fine dense rock sometimes called clinkstone. This is a volcanic rock found most commonly in North Dakota, Colorado and Germany.

Rack for hanging "is forty-four inches by twenty-two inches, which is the size I can carry in the car trunk in a box made 'specially for it."

Soft cotton string for hanging rocks

Screw eyes

Masonry bit

Drill

3 mallets

TO MAKE

In Mary's words:

"We were picnicking and came upon this deposit of phonolite and we carried it home for a wind chime for the patio. My husband drilled the holes with a hard masonry bit. The holes did not change the tones. The strings holding the rocks are plain cotton wrapping string—best to preserve the vibrations.

"As the rocks tinkled in the wind, I realized there were many tones and became curious if it would be possible to find a scale. After three years of tapping rocks I came up with the instrument as it is at present. The rocks are all natural and have not been cut."

TO PLAY

The one mallet in the right hand plays the melody. Use two mallets in the left hand for harmony.

Other Varieties of Rock Instruments

Use your imagination!

MATERIALS

Use any of the following:
Heavy plate glass
Thin slabs of fine-grained marble
Rhyolite, a volcanic stone found in the Palisades of the Hudson River and Devil's Post Pile, California
Other volcanic type rock such as obsidian and gneiss
Stones from northern Scotland are incorporated into an instrument owned by the Metropolitan Museum of Art in New York.
Nephrite, as used in the Heavenly Temple in Peking, China

TO MAKE

Each type will be different. Use the same assembly principles as given for the Wooden Xylophones (page 92). The largest rock should be the lowest tone. The rocks will progressively get smaller—test each for tone. Rocks *may* be tuned by chipping, but there is great risk of cracking the whole piece. A small rock may be made about 1 step lower by taking a small chip from the middle of the rock (making it thinner).

HINTS

A standard wood xylophone frame in a semi-rectangular shape is the easiest to make. Just be sure to have two thin strips of insulating materials covering the wood so the tone bars (rocks) will vibrate freely.

Flower Pot Bells

They even look like bells.

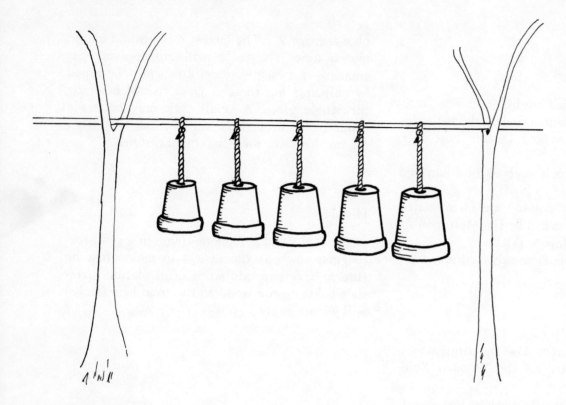

MATERIALS

5 unglazed clay flower pots, of different sizes (A)

Five ¼" dowels in 2" lengths, or five 1½" nails

Heavy cord or wrapping twine, approximately 60"

1 pole or dowel, 36" long, for hanging

Wooden mallet, for playing

TO MAKE

1. Select pots for tone by tapping. Remember that size alone does not determine tone; thickness of pot is also important.

A

2. Cut cord into 12" lengths.
3. Tie each length of cord around a 2" dowel or nail. Thread each through the hole in the bottom of a pot.
4. Suspend from pole like bells.

HINT

Play gently—clay pots are more fragile than they look. One crack may destroy the sound.

Bottles

A wonderful way to use empty bottles is to play them! In reviewing a concert, the San Francisco Chronicle, *June 6, 1975, said, "The witty songs are set against the lacy overleaf of the piano with occasional help from a ukulele, Scotch, wine and Coke bottles and a fine old tin washtub."*

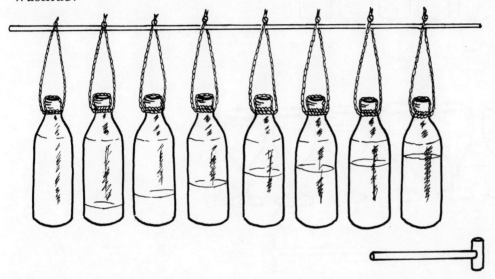

MATERIALS

8 glass bottles chosen for clear bright tones (soft drink, wine or beer bottles work nicely)
Heavy cord or wrapping twine
Pole or dowel, about 36″ long
Wooden mallet for playing

TO MAKE

1. Line up the bottles.
2. Use an empty bottle for the lowest tone and fill the others from a pitcher of water, tapping as you add water to test for the desired tone (A).
3. Lay a 2′ length of cord across the top of each bottle (B).
4. Wrap a small cord around the neck of bottle, catching the long cord; tie tightly to hold cords in place (C).
5. Tie a firm knot at the top of the long cord and slip pole through for suspending.

TO PLAY

With a mallet, pick out your favorite tune, and play.

Glasses

The quality of the crystal determines the quality of the sound.

MATERIALS

8 drinking glasses or 8 wine glasses
Wooden mallet for playing

TO MAKE

1. Line up glasses.
2. Fill glasses with water to achieve the desired tones. Use an empty glass for the lowest tone.

TO PLAY

Tap the sides of the glasses at about the water line. Do this gently, for the glasses are fragile. Fine blown wine glasses can be played by rubbing a damp finger around the rims of the glasses. The delicate vibrations of the glass make a singing tone.

HINT

Two people can play harmony if two sets of glasses are tuned alike.

Ice Cream Stick Thumb Piano

Ice cream or craft sticks or bamboo reeds add rhythm but have less tone than metal.

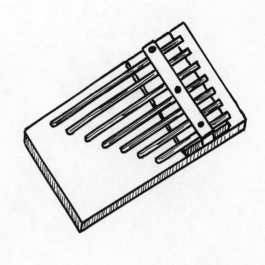

MATERIALS

One 5" x 7" piece of ½" plywood
7 ice cream or craft sticks or bamboo strips
Two 1" x 5" x ½" pieces of wood
¼" x 5" x ½" piece of wood
3 screws, each 1" long
4 nails
Hammer
Saw
Screwdriver

TO MAKE

1. With the saw, cut a 5" x 7" piece out of the ½" plywood.
2. Cut two 1" x 5" x ½" and one ¼" x 5" x ½" strips of wood.
3. Nail the two 1" x 5" strips of wood to the 5" x 7" plywood base, placing one 1" from the end of the base, and the other ½" from the first (A).
4. With the saw, cut the craft sticks or bamboo strips into pieces of regularly decreasing length.
5. Evenly space sticks across the 1" strips of wood (B); the longest stick will make the lowest tone.
6. Place the ¼" x 5" x ½" strip of wood over the sticks, centering it between the two 1" x 5" strips (see photograph).
7. Screw strip in place between the sticks, adjusting sticks to tones desired.

TO PLAY

Hold instrument with both hands, free ends of sticks facing you, and gently pluck the tone bars (sticks) with the thumbs.

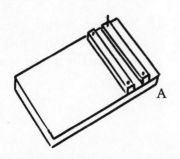

A

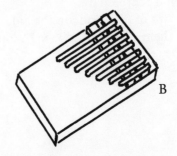

B

Tuned Thumb Piano

A more sophisticated variation that can be tuned to the scale of your choice. Traditionally the middle tones are the lowest ones. The highest tones are on each end.

MATERIALS

One 12″ x 8″ piece of ⅛″ plywood
One 8″ x ⅜″ dowel
One 4″ x ¼″ dowel
White glue
Saw
10 coping saw blades or 30″ flat spring steel wire
Sandpaper
Tinsnips
2 screws, each 1″ long
Drill
Screwdriver

TO MAKE

1. With saw, cut the plywood as shown in the cutting diagram (A).
2. With a 1″ drill, make a hole in one of the 5″ x 4″ x 7″ pieces of plywood, 1½″ up from the 5″ width of the box and centered (B).
3. The two 7″ x 1″ strips of plywood are the sides of the box. Glue them to the 5″ x 4″ x 7″ top and bottom (C). Dry thoroughly.
4. Glue the 1″ x 4¾″ piece of plywood to the wide end of the box, and the 1″ x 3¾″ piece to the narrow end of the box (D). Dry thoroughly.
5. Cut two 4″ pieces from the ⅜″ dowel. Glue one of these dowels ½″ from the narrow end of box.
6. Glue the 4″ length of ¼″ dowel 1¼″ from the ⅜″ dowel (E). Dry thoroughly.
7. With the tinsnips, cut the coping saw blades, making the shortest 2½″ for high tones and varying the length by about ¼″ for each tone, with the lowest tone in the center of the box.
8. Lay blades (tone bars) across dowels and space evenly.
9. Drill a hole close to each end of the second 4″ length of ⅜″ dowel. Use a bit the same size as the screws to be used. Place this dowel over tone bars (blades) and screw tightly in place (F).
10. To tune thumb piano, loosen screws and slide the tone bars back or forward to achieve the proper tone. Tighten.

Hold instrument with both hands and gently pluck the tone bars with the thumbs.

Some varieties are made with large wooden sound boxes on legs. The tone bars can be quite long and up to 2″ thick. Other varieties have vibrating disks attached to the wood.

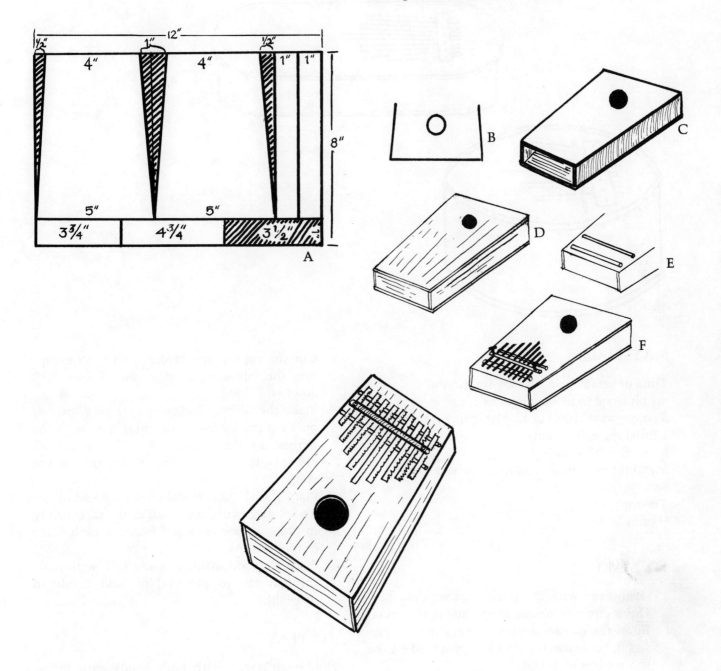

Tin Can Thumb Piano

A variation of the native gourd or coconut thumb piano made with imported sardine or tuna can. Save the lid for a pattern piece.

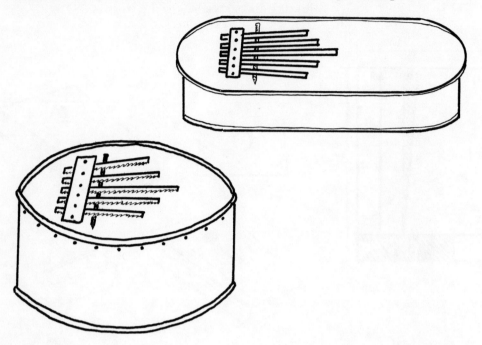

MATERIALS

Tuna or sardine can tin, not aluminum
¼″ plywood to fit the top of can
3 coping saw blades or 12″ flat spring steel wire
1 finishing nail, 2″ long
Small finishing nails, ½″ long
Metal lid from tuna can or sardine can
Saw
Tinsnips
Hammer

TO MAKE

1. Open cans with can opener rather than key. Cut a circle or oblong shape, using the metal lid of the can for a pattern, from the ¼″ plywood, being careful not to cut yourself on the sharp edges of the lid.
2. With the tinsnips, cut a ½″ x 3″ strip from the metal lid.
3. Cut the coping saw blades with the tinsnips into the following lengths: one 3″, two 2½″, and two 2″ long.
4. Place the 2″-long finishing nail on plywood; position cut blades on finishing nail, with the longest in the center, the 2½″ lengths on either side of it and the 2″ lengths on the ends.
5. Place the ½″ x 3″ metal strip over end of cut blades and, with the small nails, tack firmly in place, at the ends and between each blade or tone bar (A).
6. Place plywood inside can and tack with nails through can to plywood to hold firmly in place (B).

TO PLAY

Hold instrument with both hands with unfastened ends of tone bars facing you, and gently pluck the tone bars with the thumbs.

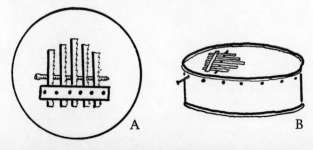

A   B

Coconut Thumb Piano

The thumb piano originated in the African Congo at least five hundred years ago. It is made in over a hundred varieties and known by many names—zanza, mbira, kalimba or Kaffir harp. A relative of the xylophone, it may be tuned to any five-tone scale or to the standard eight-tone Western scale. The steel blades play separate notes, and are gently depressed and released with the thumbs of both hands; thus, the name thumb piano.

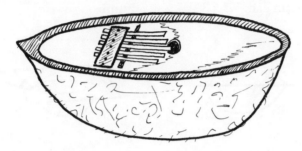

MATERIALS

1 coconut
Crayon
Saw
3 coping saw blades or 8″ flat spring steel wire
Sandpaper
Metal from tin can
Finishing nail, 2″ long
Small finishing nails, ½″ long
Drill, hand or electric
¼″ plywood to fit top of coconut half
White glue
Tinsnips
Scissors

Sheet of paper
Tape
Hammer

TO MAKE

1. With the saw, cut the coconut in half lengthwise (A).
2. Let coconut dry until meat shrinks away from the sides of shell. Remove meat. (See Methods and Materials section.)
3. Place a sheet of paper over top of half of coconut and with a crayon rub the inside edges of the shell to get a pattern (B). Cut out pattern with scissors.

Thumb Pianos: Sardine Can (left), Tunafish Can (center), Coconut (right).

4. Tape pattern on plywood and with the saw cut out the shape. This is the best time for fitting—making sure the plywood will fit snugly in the top of the coconut. Sometimes a little sanding will help make it fit more easily.

5. Drill a hole about ½" diameter, centered in the plywood, for sound.

6. Cut the coping saw blades with the tinsnips into 3", 2½" and 2" lengths.

7. Cut a metal strip from the tin can, ½" x 3".

8. Place a 2"-long finishing nail on plywood and line up the metal blades across it. Place ½" x 3" metal strip over end of blades and nail in place (C).

9. Glue plywood in coconut (D).

TO PLAY

Hold instrument by cupping in hands and gently depress and release the tone bars with your thumbs.

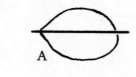

A

B

C

D

Wood Block—Slit Drum

The hollow resonating chamber gives a crisp, sharp sound.

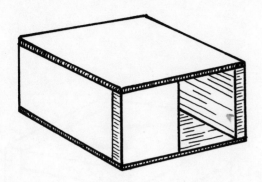

MATERIALS

24″ x 3¼″ x 1″ pine
6¾″ x 9″ x ⅛″ plywood
White glue
Saw
Drumsticks or mallets

TO MAKE

1. Cut two 6″ lengths from the 3¼″ wood.
2. Cut two 2½″ lengths from the 3¼″ wood.
3. Cut one 5⅛″ length from the 3¼″ wood.
4. Cut 2 pieces, each 4⅛″ x 6¾″, from the plywood.
5. Follow diagram and glue the lengths of pine onto one piece of plywood.

6. Glue second piece of plywood on top. Dry thoroughly.

TO PLAY

Tap with drumsticks or mallets.

HINTS

A primitive and easy substitute for the above box is a length of hollow bamboo. Cut on either side of two joints (nodes), leaving the tube solid on both ends. A ¼″ slit cut along half of the length will allow the sound waves to escape.

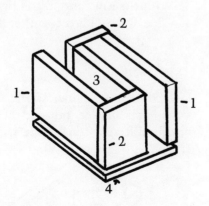

Box Drum

First came the hollow log. Then the large slit drum, which evolved into this portable version. Fine hardwood makes a much better sound than plywood.

MATERIALS

4 pieces of wood, each 6″ x 8″. Hardwoods have a very nice sound. Any size will work nicely.

Saw. A coping saw is best, for the blade can be removed for cutting the inside shapes.

Pencil

Drill

Twelve 1½″ finishing nails

Hammer

White glue

Mallet or drumstick(s)

TO MAKE

1. Draw patterns on wood (see diagram A).
2. Drill holes at each angle of each pattern; this is for inserting saw blade.
3. With the saw, cut on the lines drawn.
4. Glue and nail box together (B).

TO PLAY

Lay box on any side. Using one or two drumsticks or a mallet, tap the different areas of the box for different tonal patterns.

A

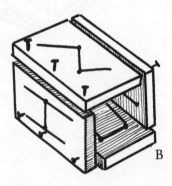

B

Water Drum ("Jicara de Agua")

Especially simple, this is an unusually effective drum from Mexico.

MATERIALS

1 gourd about 9″ in diameter, or ½ of a large
   coconut
Metal washtub
Water
Stick for drumming

TO PLAY

Place about 2″ of water in the bottom of shallow washtub. Place hollow side of gourd or coconut down in the pan. Tap the gourd or coconut with the stick.

HINT

This is very effective as an ethnic or cultural presentation with the Yaqui Indian Raspador (see page 30).

Wooden Xylophones

In any version a xylophone is one of the most useful and enjoyable instruments you can make. It is well worth the time and effort to tune it properly. Choose your wood carefully, for tone quality varies. The best wood is rosewood from South America; black walnut and maple are also very good. While mahogany, gum and birch are all acceptable, redwood and clear pine will be only fair in tonal quality. A general rule for the best sound: All tone bars should be the same width, and ½" thick.

Wood—approximate sizes:

Middle C—12"	G—10¼"
D—11½"	A—9¾"
E—11"	B—9¼"
F—10¾"	C—9"

TO MAKE

1. Cut the lowest tone first; this will be the longest stick.
2. Lay the bar on a piece of rope placed in a "U" shape (A) on a hard surface. (This is a temporary frame.) Tap lightly. Compare the sound with middle C on a piano. If too low, cut a very small slice off end of bar. Continue in this manner until you achieve desired tone. Remember all wood differs in tone. Even two equal pieces of the same wood may differ. We have several samples, all tuned to middle C, and their measurements differ from 3" to 5".
3. Raise the tone by shortening with a saw or a file, depending on the size of cut needed. If you have raised the tone too much, you may be able to lower it by making a ¼" cut, to begin with, underneath the bar, parallel to the end. Only trial and error will tune the instrument. Each individual instrument will vary.

MATERIALS

Saw
File
Sandpaper
Rope for preliminary sounding
Racks and mallets of your choice. (See instructions below.)

TO PLAY

Tap with a light bounce. The type of mallet you use will change the quality of the tone.

HINTS

There are definite advantages in *not* fixing the bars of a xylophone in place permanently. Many songs from around the world may be played in different scales, which may be set up when the tone bars can be changed. The Orf-Schulwerk music method, for example, makes special use of the pentatonic scales to stimulate creativity and group music.

RACKS FOR XYLOPHONES

1. Table racks may be made from any size wood, depending on the instrument. We used 1" x 2" pine (B), two pieces 16" long, one 5" and one 7", to make the table rack shown (C). It is important to keep the tone bars up and apart so they can vibrate freely. Tone bars may be kept apart by gluing small rectangles of the padding used on the rack between the bars. The wood may be padded with any of the following: stick-on foam weather stripping; thin strips of plastic foam; felt, carpet or carpet padding strips; soft cotton rope. (One child's instrument frame is made entirely of 1½" foam rubber. It is easily folded into a box when the music time is over.)

2. For hanging racks, use small screw eyes in the tops of the wooden bars. Attach wrapping twine or sturdy cord through screw eyes and attach to dowel or hang from pole (D).

3. For rope ladders, use a good quality but soft two-ply rope. Lay the rope in an upside-down "V" shape with at least one more foot of rope on each side than you expect the instrument to use, for hanging. Untwist a 2" section on each side of the rope near the bottom of the "V" and insert the largest bar (E). The rope will hold the bar at each side. Leave about 1" in between each bar and continue in this manner until the scale is all inserted (F).

4. You may use either soft or hard mallets, or both. See the section in the drum chapter that follows for more elaborate ideas. For simple mallets, you may use a professional drumstick (G); a Tinkertoy knob and stick (H); a wooden drawer knob glued to a ¼" dowel about 10" long; or a small hard rubber ball speared on a ¼" dowel (I).

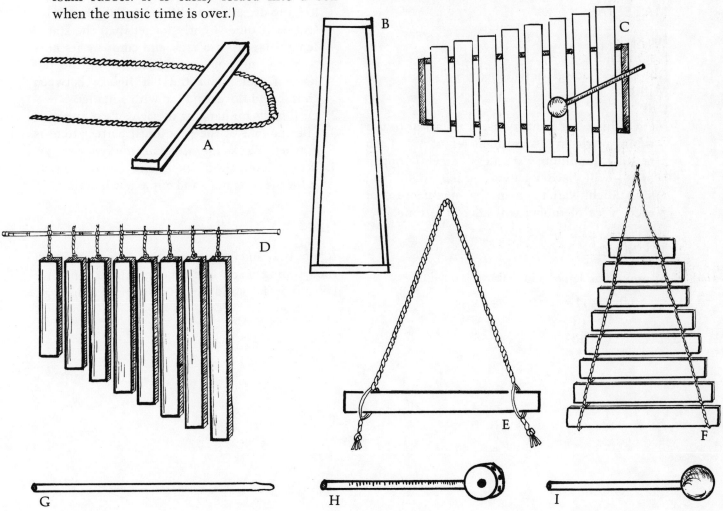

Metal Tubing Xylophones

The tones of a metal xylophone are generally more appealing than a wooden one, but the metal makes the construction harder and more expensive.

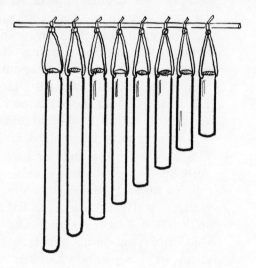

MATERIALS

Hacksaw
Flat metal file
One 1″ x 36″ dowel for hanging
Mallet
Drill
Metal tubing. For ordinary use it is easiest to use tubing with an inside diameter of ½″. Each metal—aluminum, stainless steel, copper, brass—will have its own special sound and size. Slight variations in the manufacture of each piece of tubing will affect the tone.

TO MAKE

Approximate lengths for tubing:

High C—11⅝″	G—9⁷⁄₁₆″
D—10¹⁵⁄₁₆″	A—8⅞″
E—10¼″	B—8⁷⁄₁₆″
F—9⅞″	C—8⅛″

(Refer to directions for Wooden Xylophones.)

1. Cut each tube slightly longer than the stated length, lay it on a rack and compare its note to the same note on a piano. If you do not have a rack, hold the bar lightly between thumb and finger and tap with a mallet.
2. Drill holes for hanging in each side of tube.
3. File the end of the tube until correct tone is reached. Work *carefully and slowly.*
4. If tube is too short (its note is too sharp), save it for the next note and cut a new length.

HINT

Again, trial and error and patience are needed for good tuning. Each instrument will be different. For other racks and mallets, see preceding page.

Metal Gongs and Triangles

Important signals for body and spirit come from the Chinese temple gong and the Western chuckwagon dinner bell.

MATERIALS

To obtain the metal odds and ends required to make these, you must take your wooden mallet and go through an old barn, an ironmonger's shop or the hardware store. The type of metal is all-important to the desired sound. Solid brass, iron or steel is best. Longer length gives larger and deeper vibrations.

TO MAKE

Suspend your metal finding with rope through a small hole to allow the metal to vibrate freely.

TO PLAY

Strike with metal for a bright sound, or strike with a padded wooden mallet for a more muffled sound.

SUGGESTED TYPES

Long iron bar suspended through an eye at the top

Long iron bar bent into a triangle by a blacksmith; this shape makes it possible to play three tones quickly

West Indies "Las Sartenes," a set of heavy iron frying pans suspended from a rack

African-type bells made by removing clapper from a heavy metal bell or a cow bell

Brass or steel pipe suspended by a heavy cord

Quick and Simple

1. Cymbals. Two pot lids; tie ribbons to the handles for colorful decoration (A).
2. Triangles. Suspend large screw eyes from a soft cord or yarn. Tie the other end of cord to small nail for striking (B).
3. Slit drum. Hollow out a wooden block from the preschool or kindergarten (C).
4. Thumb piano. Clamp ice cream sticks to a table with a ruler and "C" clamps (D).
5. Jugs. Use a collection of jugs, glasses or bottles of different tone qualities (E).
6. Castanets. For easier playing of purchased castanets: Remove string. Place castanets back-to-back, and thread a loop of elastic through the holes. Knot (F). Turn to original position (G). Elastic will make a spring.
7. Coconut shell. Saw coconut in half (see Materials and Methods section), and drill holes for attaching heavy cord or yarn (H). Clack halves together or tap separately on a table. They can be used to imitate horses' hooves or tapped just for rhythm.
8. Ili-ili (Hawaiian castanets). Two smooth, flat stones are held in one hand and clicked together (I). Very effective, but it takes practice.
9. Tone bells. Suspend a collection of nails, keys, tubes (wood or metal), or even silverware from a small frame (J).

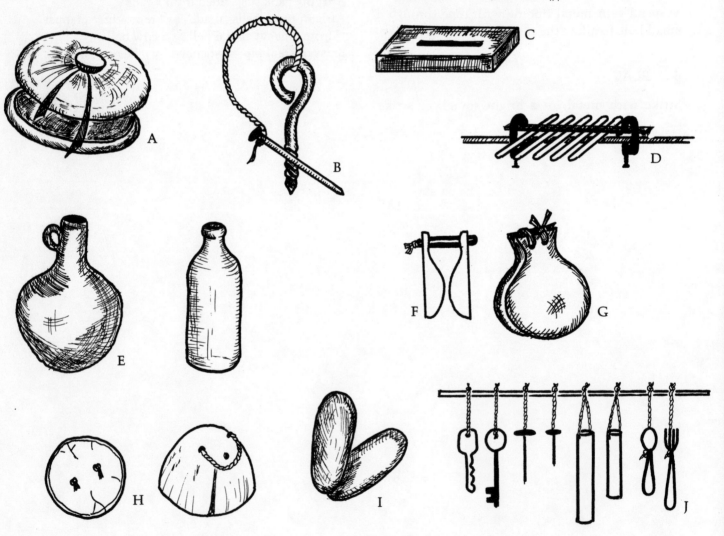

Drums and Vibrating Membranes

History

Whether the sound comes from a Hopi Snake Dance, a frenetic rock group, or Brahms' First Symphony, there is an instant reaction to the sound of beating drums. Very few listeners will be able to ignore a steady drumbeat. Most people will become excited, although some will be disturbed. Drums were used in ancient Greece and they were a favored instrument on the American Continent before Columbus arrived. In some African tribes, drums are carved like human figures, with the female being the larger. They are believed to have the power to communicate with the gods and the dead. In one area, the king had absolute power over everything but the royal drums. The Indian medicine man's drum calls the gods' attention to important events and summons them to heal the sick.

Why does the rhythmic beat of a drum have such an effect on our breathing, pulse rate and our whole nervous system? There are two possible reasons. First, our own heart beats an accompaniment to the ebb and flow of our emotions and our body responds to this echo of our heartbeat. Second, the beginning months of our lives are spent in a soft dark world beneath a steadily beating heart and those early experiences may be brought back by another rhythmic beat. Rhythm is used to mark special events all our lives: religious ceremonies, love songs, patriotic marches. And who can forget the slow drum cadence of the funeral cortege of young President Kennedy?

A true drum is one in which the sound is produced by striking a thin membrane stretched over a hollow chamber. It is impossible to list all the materials that have been used to make drums. They are usually made from wood, but they may be made from ceramic, metal or a hole in the ground. The frame is usually round but it sounds almost the same if it is square. Several drums made from human skulls are shown in the Metropolitan Museum of Art in New York.

Drums can be roughly classified into three groups. The open drum has a head, but the bottom of the frame is open. This tambourine-like drum is often lightweight and portable. It is a favorite of many American Indian tribes and is often called a war drum because it was light enough to be carried into battle. The Eskimo someak is made from thin, fragile caribou skin, and is struck only on the wood or whalebone frame.

A closed drum has a head, and the hollow chamber is closed. The symphonic kettle drum is a refined version of the closed drum. The American Indians have a water drum which is a closed drum about one-quarter full of water. The water augments the sound and carries it farther. The original drum was made of wood with a bunghole for adjusting the water level. When the Indians saw the large iron stew kettle of the pioneers they quickly adapted it as a practical vessel for food and for music. The empty lard pail and the rubber inner tube are recent substitutions and the sound is remarkably good. This last version has been popular for the past fifty years and is used today by many tribes in the Southwest.

A double-headed drum has a membrane on both sides. The big bass drum of the marching band is an example. Most elaborate ceremonial drums are made with two heads. Africa probably has more drums than any other continent, including an hour-glass type of drum, which has a unique set of strings that control the tone of the drum through the pressure of the musician's arm. An expert drummer from Senegal can actually talk with his drum.

Drums in Western cultures are usually made to be played with "beaters." While the American Indian almost always uses one, other cultures prefer the use of hands in a technique equal in complexity to that of the concert pianist. The small tabla from India have many tones in the center, edge and frame. To make these sounds all parts of both hands are used.

One unusual type of drum is called a friction drum. The skin top is vibrated by the movement of a stick through a small hole in the drumhead. The Dutch adaptation of this drum is especially interesting (see page 112).

The whirling bull roarer is not a drum, not a stringed instrument, but is included here because the sound comes from the thin vibrating string. It is well known all over the world and is used as a child's toy and also as a representation of supernatural voices (see page 114).

The Navajo Indians have a chant, a prayer, which follows the slow beat of the drum:

> *May I walk with beauty before me.*
> *May I walk with beauty behind me.*
> *May I walk with beauty below me.*
> *May I walk with beauty above me.*
> *With beauty all around me, may I walk.*
>
> *[Adapted]*

Unusual Drums

There are many unusual drums easily adapted for outdoor musical occasions.

THE MAIDU FOOT DRUM

A concave log half (or a board) is placed over a trench in the ground and played by stamping feet. The skin drum was not used by the earliest California Indians.

THE APACHE "EXTRA" DRUM

A whole cow skin over a springy bed of green branches (one foot high) accommodates extra drummers who want to play along with the formal ceremonial drums.

THE AFRICAN GROUND DRUM

An animal skin is pegged over a circular hole in the ground. This type of drum probably evolved into the "mosquito drum" which became the washtub bass—this will be discussed in the string section.

THE SUBSTITUTE SLAVE DRUM

A heavy stick thumped against a wooden floor became a substitute drum in early times when skin-head drums were banned by some slave owners who feared voodoo organization. The islands off the coast of Georgia were relatively isolated until recently, and they have retained some of the antebellum music. The Georgia Sea Island Singers used this "drum," a tambourine, and their clapping hands to create an evening filled with rhythm in their concerts at a group of California universities a few years ago. (See References: Jones and Hawes, *Step It Down.*)

Rawhide Tom-Tom

The ceremonial drum was most important in the native music of America and Africa. The lightweight version below requires some skill and patience but it is effective as well as attractive.

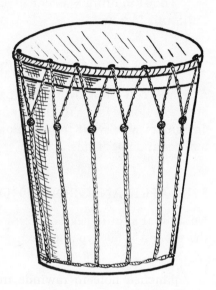

MATERIALS

One 3-gallon plastic pot. (Nurseries use these for potted shrubs and trees; usually they will give you one.)

Rawhide, at least 3″ wider than the diameter of the pot

Bamboo or a green branch about ¼″ thick, and long enough to go around the top of the pot

Needle and thread, for whipping bamboo onto rawhide. (We used regular heavy-duty sewing thread and needle.)

String, for tying rawhide to pot

Needle, large enough to thread string through

Pencil

Scissors

Drill

Punch

Beads

TO MAKE

1. With the drill, make holes in the base of the plastic pot (A). We used 18 holes evenly spaced around the base.

2. Thread string onto large needle, tie a heavy knot in one end and start on the inside of the pot. Come up through one hole and down through the next hole. From the inside of the pot, come up through the third hole and back down through to the second, then up through the fourth and down through the third, etc. (B). What you are doing is making

a continuous tight string around the base of pot to hold the beaded string. Continue in this manner until there is string all around the base (be sure to come all the way back to the first two holes). Knot.

3. Place the open end of the pot on the rawhide and draw around it with a pencil. This gives you a guideline for punching holes and for sewing the bamboo.
4. Place the rawhide in cool water for about 1 hour, or until soft.
5. When soft, dry the rawhide with a towel just enough to prevent dripping while you are working with it.
6. Cut a circle (this can be done with regular scissors) 1½" wider all around than the penciled pot opening.
7. With the punch make holes (the same number as in the base) around the penciled circle, making sure they are evenly spaced (C).
8. With the needle and thread, whip the bamboo (or branch) onto the very edge of the rawhide, bending the bamboo to fit the circle (D).
9. Place the rawhide over the top of the pot.
10. Thread string on large needle. Insert into punched hole in rawhide from the top and down the outside of the pot, leaving a loose end for knotting later. Slip on a bead, slip

needle through string at bottom of pot and come back up through the same bead. Slip string through next hole in rawhide, again from the top, and continue in this manner around drum (E).
11. When you have gone completely around the drum, tie the two loose ends in a temporary holding knot, then adjust the string, going all around the drum and pulling it as taut as you can. Retie the ends in a permanent knot, pulling tightly. The rawhide should remain damp while you are working with it. If it should begin to dry, spray it with water or sprinkle it to keep it flexible. When the rawhide dries it will shrink and pull the string even tighter.
12. The beater in the photograph is a padded leather beater, as shown in Diagram F, page 115.

TO PLAY

Use a beater, Indian style, or play with your hands, African style.

HINT

See Methods and Materials section for working with rawhide.

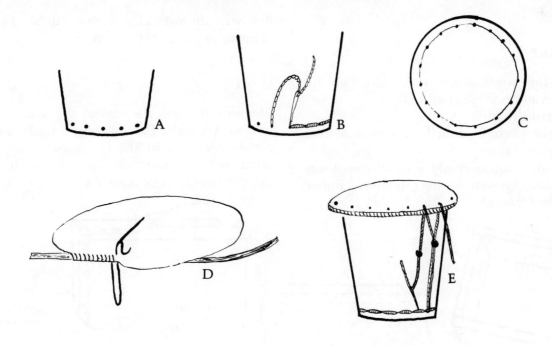

Square Hand Drum

Square drums were commonly used by the Indians of the Northwest United States. The box-shaped frame is much easier to make than a round one.

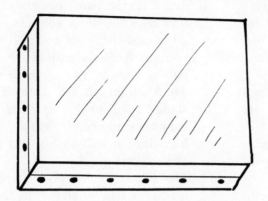

MATERIALS

1 piece of wood, 1″ x 1¾″ x 54″. This is for a drum about 12″ x 15″—amount of wood needed varies, of course, with the size of the drum.

Nails for making frame (we used 8)

Rawhide, a piece large enough to cover frame completely

Upholstery tacks

Hammer

Saw

Scissors

TO MAKE

1. With the saw, cut the wood into two 12″ lengths and two 15″ lengths.
2. Nail frame together (A).
3. Soak the rawhide for at least 1 hour in cool water, until soft.
4. Trim the rawhide evenly with scissors, keeping it large enough to wrap completely around the drum frame.

5. Using the tacks, hammer the rawhide to one edge of the frame (B).
6. Pull the rawhide completely around the frame, overlapping the first row of tacks. Tack rawhide down, keeping it taut (C).
7. Cut a corner out of the rawhide so that the edge will lie flat (D). Fold over frame and tack in place.

TO PLAY

Beat with drumsticks or with hands, to the beat of music or just a rhythmic beat.

HINT

The only limit to the size of this drum is the rawhide available. The covering of fabric and airplane dope used in the following round hand drum could be substituted for rawhide, although the skin head is more resonant.

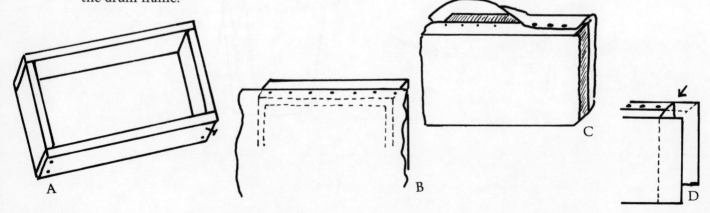

A   B   C   D

Round Hand Drum

Made with fabric and airplane dope, this is a simple and rather pleasant-sounding drum. It can be made quickly, too. Airplane dope is a varnish-like product used to coat fabric; it can be purchased at lumber stores.

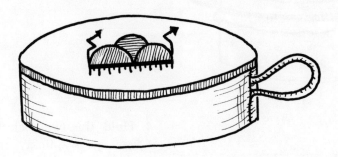

MATERIALS

1 large, round, shallow (3") tin (the type used for fruitcake and candy)

Fabric, 2" larger than diameter of tin (lightweight muslin, percale)

Strong rubber bands

Wrapping twine for tying

3½ oz. airplane dope. (Note the danger markings on the bottle.)

Brush for applying dope

Leather or fabric to cover sides of tin. (If fabric is used, you may want a band of leather to cover the fabric edge—see finished diagram.)

Pencil

Oil pastels (optional)

TO MAKE

1. Remove bottom from tin. For a smooth edge, use an electric can opener, if available.

2. Place tin on fabric and trace around.
3. Cut fabric 2" wider all around than marked line.
4. Dampen fabric, place over tin and secure tightly with a rubber band. Adjust fullness of fabric evenly. Tie tightly with wrapping twine (A).
5. Pull fabric as tight as possible.
6. Dry thoroughly.
7. With the brush, paint fabric with 3 coats of airplane dope. Dry thoroughly between each coat.
8. Finish sides with a band of leather or fabric, adding a loop for holding.
9. Paint a design on drumhead with oil pastels for an attractive appearance (optional).

TO PLAY

Use an easy, bouncing stroke with a light beater.

Paper and Cloth Drumheads

Shellac and a grocery bag can substitute for rawhide.

MATERIALS

Heavy brown grocery bag
Cheesecloth, 4″ wider than drum frame
Pencil
Rubber band
Shellac
Brush
Wrapping twine
Coffee can or fruitcake can for drum frame
Can opener

TO MAKE

1. Lay cheesecloth over brown paper. (Treat as one piece from here on.)
2. Center drum frame over fabric and draw around it (A).
3. Cut the fabric (drumhead) 2″ large than circle drawn.

4. Hold the cheesecloth/paper circles together and pass quickly under running water to dampen cloth.
5. With cheesecloth uppermost, lay circles over top of can. Hold in place with a rubber band and adjust the fullness around the edge of can.
6. Tie tightly with wrapping twine. Leave a loop for holding drum if desired (B).
7. Dry thoroughly.
8. Apply three coats of shellac (more if desired), allowing head to dry between each coat.
9. With a can opener, open the bottom of the can for a more resonant sound.

HINT

White glue or rubber cement may be used instead of shellac but they are not as strong nor as resonant.

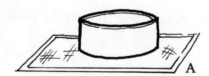

Apache Water Drum

"One small piece of turquoise and one small stone must be put in the water of the drum," our Apache friend said.

MATERIALS

Metal bucket or can with a pronounced rim

Rubber inner tube section larger than the top of the bucket. (For a small drum use a thin tube, for a large drum use a truck tube.)

Strip of rubber inner tube, ½" wide and at least twice the circumference of the drum, for tying head

Pencil

Length of strong cord

12" length of string

Heavy scissors

Beater, traditionally the circular branch type

TO MAKE

1. Cut a section from an inner tube at least 4" larger all around than top of bucket. Split tube on inside seam so it will lie flat.
2. Place opening of bucket on inner tube and trace around with a pencil for a pattern (A). Following this shape, cut 4" beyond the pencil marking. This will give border room for tying.
3. Pour water into the bucket, to about ¼ of the depth of the bucket (B).

The following steps are best done with one or two people to help:

4. Make a loop at the end of the ½"-wide rubber strip and fasten it with cord. Tie a 12" piece of string securely to the other end of the rubber strip, leaving an 8" piece extending from the knot, for use later (C).
5. With four strong hands stretch the rubber head very tightly over the bucket. Pull the rubber tie through the loop (D) and stretch it tightly around the drumhead to hold it securely in place. Adjust the folds in the drumhead as you go along. With the 8" piece of string, tie the ½" rubber strip in place as tightly as possible (E).

TO PLAY

Strike with a firm but bounding touch. The spring of the circular beater (see Diagram L on page 115) is ideal for this drum.

HINTS

The water can be omitted for a more practical but softer-sounding drum. The head must be very tight to give a good sound. Try your local service station for inner tubes they may have to give away, before you buy.

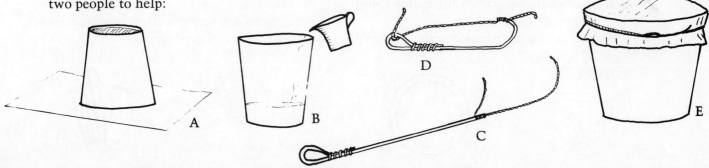

Coconut Bongo Drums

An attractive and compelling instrument.

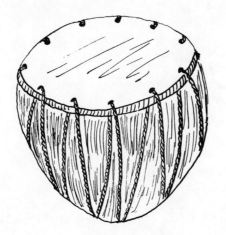

MATERIALS

1 large coconut
Saw
Pencil
Rawhide, large enough to cover coconut
Heavy wrapping twine and needle large enough
   to thread it through
Bamboo (a bamboo skewer will work nicely)
Needle and thread
Punch

TO MAKE

1. With the saw, cut the coconut ⅔ up from one end (A). Use the larger piece.
2. Dry coconut and remove meat (see Methods and Materials section).
3. Place the open end of coconut on the rawhide and draw around with a pencil. This gives you a guideline for punching holes and for sewing the bamboo.
4. Place the rawhide in cool water for 1 hour, or until soft.
5. Remove moisture from rawhide with a towel, to prevent dripping while working.
6. Cut a circle about 1" larger than marked.
7. With the punch, make holes in the rawhide along the penciled guideline (B), making sure they are evenly spaced.
8. With the needle and thread, whip the bamboo onto the very edge of the rawhide, bending the bamboo to make a circle (C).
9. Place the rawhide over top of coconut.
10. Make a circle 2" in diameter out of the wrapping twine and place it on the bottom of coconut. (Sometimes cellophane tape will help to hold it in place while you are working.)
11. Thread twine on a large needle. Insert needle from the top through punched hole in the rawhide, down the side of the coconut, loop it around the circle of twine at the base. Bring it back up and through the rawhide, again from the top (D). Continue in this manner until you have gone completely around the coconut. Tie a temporary knot at the two loose ends. Go around the drum again, pulling the twine as taut as you can. Retie the knot. The rawhide should be damp while working. If it should dry, spray with water to keep it flexible.

TO PLAY

The bongo drums are played by tapping the rawhide with the hands or fingers.

HINT

These drums are very effective, especially if you have about three of varying sizes.

A

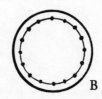

B

C

D

Hourglass Drum

Many tone changes are possible with this drum, the original of which was carved from wood in Africa. Pressure against the strings tightens the drumhead and raises the tone. Using coconut substitutes for wood, we found that our version of the drum has several tones, too.

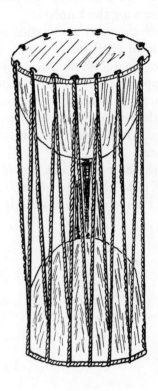

Hourglass Drum, Coconut Bongo Drum.

MATERIALS

2 large coconuts
Saw
Rawhide
Pencil
Bamboo
Twine
Needle and thread
5″-long piece of 1¼″ dowel
Drill

2 screws, each 1″ long
Punch

TO MAKE

1. With the saw, cut each coconut ⅔ up from one end (A). Use the two larger pieces.
2. Dry coconut and remove meat (see Materials and Methods section).

110

3. With the drill, make a hole through the base of each coconut just large enough for the screw (B). Set screw in place from the inside of the coconut.

4. Drill a hole to start screw in the center of each end of the dowel. Now screw coconuts to dowel. This gives you the hourglass effect (C).

5. Place the open end of the coconut on the rawhide and draw around with a pencil. This gives you a guideline for punching holes and for sewing the bamboo.

6. Place the rawhide in cool water for about 1 hour, or until soft.

7. Remove moisture with a towel to prevent dripping while working. Cut the rawhide in a circle 1" larger than marked.

8. With the punch, make holes around the penciled circle, making sure they are evenly spaced.

9. With the needle and thread, whip the bamboo onto the edge of the rawhide, bending the bamboo to make a circle (D).

10. Repeat steps 5 through 9 for the second rawhide drumhead.

11. Place heads over coconuts. Thread a large needle with twine. Starting at the top head, go down the outside of the coconuts, and through a hole in the bottom head. Bring needle back up and go down again from the top (E), repeating until you have gone completely around the drum.

12. Holding the drum firmly, tighten the twine around the drum and knot. Wait until the rawhide is dry to drum.

TO PLAY

The drummer often plays in a crouched position with his left knee raised as a base for the drum. The pressure of his left arm and body makes the changes in tone. A short curved stick with a hard top is the traditional beater.

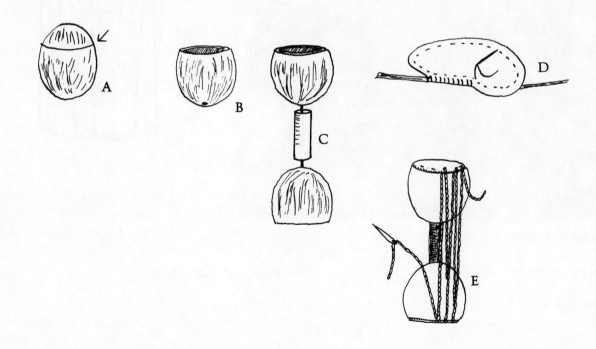

Dutch Jug Drum (Rommel Pot)

A seventeenth-century Flemish painting by Jan Molenaer, Children Making Music, *shows a child playing this friction drum. It is likely that the House of Orange, Importers, brought this drum idea back from the tropics, along with the fruit. This instrument has been part of the Christmas festivities in some areas of Holland. The drum was also called a leopard drum in Africa because of the rasping growl.*

MATERIALS

Small jug or pitcher, or a large beer stein with a
   flared rim
Large heavy balloon (traditionally a pig's bladder)
Wooden stick similar to a chopstick
Triangular file
Heavy twine
Scissors

TO MAKE

1. With the file, make notches around the wooden stick, about ⅓" apart, and along about ⅔ of the stick (A).
2. Cut off the narrow part of the balloon (B) and fit the balloon over the top of jug, pitcher or stein (C).
3. Pull balloon down tightly and tie with the twine (D).
4. Cut a ⅓" slit in the center of balloon drum head.
5. Insert notched stick.

TO PLAY

Move the stick up and down rapidly to make a loud vibration. The rasping sound of the stick is magnified by the rubber and the interior of the jug.

HINT

The native version was used in the "coming-of-age" ceremonies.

 A

 B

 C

 D

Friction Drum (Paper Version)

It is hard to believe that such a loud noise could come from a vibrating string, a toothpick and a small piece of paper. Import stores sell a version of this drum from Taiwan.

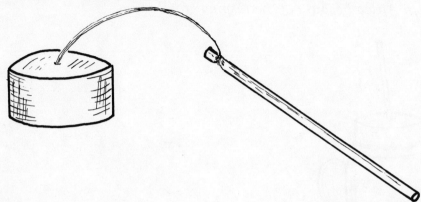

MATERIALS

1 hollow cross section of bamboo, 1¼″ in diameter by 1″ long
1 small piece of brown paper bag to cover one end of bamboo
1 toothpick
Needle
Thread, about 3 strands, 12″ long
Stick (or bamboo skewer or pencil), about 5″ long
Saw
White glue

TO MAKE

1. With the saw, cut the bamboo to a 1″ length.
2. Glue the brown paper over one end of the bamboo (A). Trim.

3. Cut the toothpick to fit inside the bamboo without touching the sides—i.e., shorter than the inside diameter of the bamboo (B).
4. Cut the stick 5″ long and notch it about ¼″ from one end (C). This is to hold the thread.
5. Thread both ends of the strands of thread on a needle and make a loop, slip it over the skewer and pull it into the notch (D).
6. With the needle, poke a hole in the center of the paper-covered bamboo and pull through. Making sure you have at least 4″ of thread from the notched stick, tie the thread to the toothpick (E).

TO PLAY

Swing, holding onto notched stick.

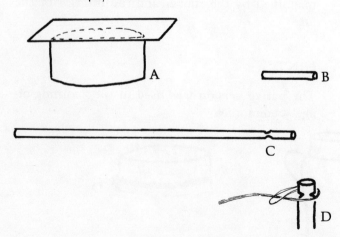

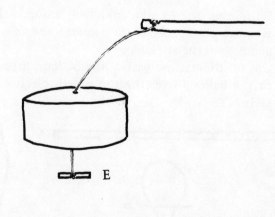

Children's Drum

Dennis the Menace keeps losing his noisy drums to Mr. Wilson. This substitute is not very loud but it looks good, and is inexpensive and durable.

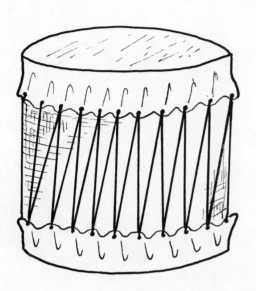

MATERIALS

1 tin can (2-lb. coffee can or large can of that size)
1 rubber inner tube (service stations usually have old ones to give away)
Punch
Twine or shoestring for lacing
Can opener

TO MAKE

1. With a can opener, cut both ends out of the can.
2. Cut inner tube open and cut two circles about 2" larger than the top and bottom of can.
3. With the punch, make holes about every 1¼" around each circle, ¾" in from the edge of the rubber (A).
4. Place one circle on table or flat surface, center can on circle and place the other circle on top (B).
5. With a long piece of twine, start at one edge and lace from top to bottom, pulling gently, all the way around the drum (C). This holds heads in place.
6. Now go around the drum again, pulling each strand tightly. When you have returned to the starting point, knot.

TO PLAY

Beat with a drumstick or hand.

HINT

This type of drum is sold in kits which require all the steps above to make, and do not sound half as good.

 A

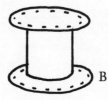 B

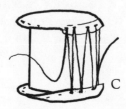 C

Bull Roarer

Ilene was a child in Arizona when she first heard a bull roarer. The summer night was black and the large Indian bonfire flared behind the strange headdresses of the Apache Crown dancers. Deep drums echoed off the canyon walls and from the darkness came the unearthly voices of the spirit world through the vibrations of bull roarers.

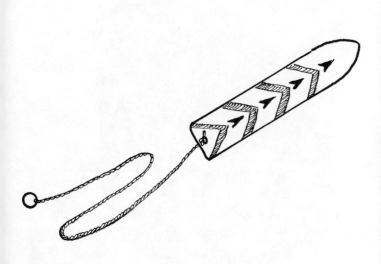

MATERIALS

1 piece of wood, ¼" x 2" x 8"
1 ring (a small drapery ring works nicely)
48" of sturdy string
Drill
Saw
Knife
Sandpaper

TO MAKE

1. With the saw, cut wood to size.
2. With the knife or saw, taper one end of the wood to a rounded point (A).
3. Sand edges.
4. With the drill, make a hole in the square end of the wood to hold the string (B).
5. Double the string to give a 24" strand. Tie the string to the ring. Put the other end through the drilled hole and tie a heavy knot. It is very important that the wood can't slip off the string.

TO PLAY

Place your finger through the ring, swing the instrument over your head and whirl it until you get a roaring sound.

HINTS

The size of the stick and the length of the cord alter the tone. The longer string has a lower pitched roar and is used by the Indians in arid climates to summon the summer thunder and rain clouds.

NOTE

The whirling sticks can be very dangerous. They should be used only in open spaces by strong, responsible hands.

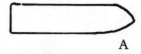

A

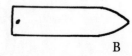

B

Drumsticks

You may use many things to beat your own drum: a new pencil with an eraser or a ceremonial stick of rawhide and feathers—or one of the suggestions below.

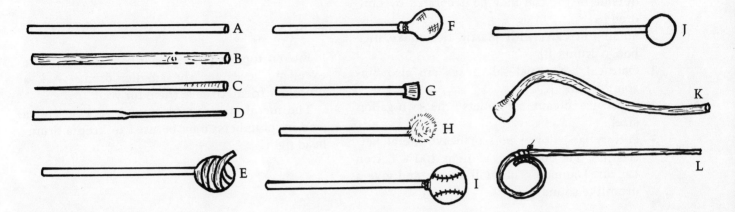

STICKS

Dowels, ¼" to ⅜" in diameter and 10" to 15" long (A), or a straight branch of similar size (B) will work nicely.

Handles from old paint brushes (C).

Chopsticks (D).

SOFT KNOBS

Strips of felt, rolled around one end of the stick. Fasten the felt to the stick with white glue, adding glue as you roll (E).

Padding of cotton or nylon stockings stuffed in chamois skin or soft leather. Use glue under padding to hold in place, and tie tightly with string or leather lacing (F).

Foam rubber or foam plastic padding, glued in place over stick and covered tightly with a heavy knit fabric (socks work nicely). Tie tightly.

Rubber crutch tips or furniture glides. Buy the tip first, then get a dowel to fit it (G).

Cork or plastic balls wound with yarn or fur (H). Use glue to hold in place.

HARD KNOBS

Cork or leather padding. Rawhide stretched over the cork or leather and stitched like a baseball is a very effective drumstick (I).

Cork or plastic balls, spools. Glue and wrap with heavy twine. Apply a coat of shellac.

Round cork floats are excellent as drum beaters (J).

African curved drumstick. Cut a green branch in the spring. Gently bend end in a half circle. Whittling the inner and outer edges of the curve makes for ease in bending. Tie with twine to hold the curve and allow· to dry. Carve knob on one curved end when dry (K).

Indian circular beater. Cut willow or similar green branch in the spring. Bend gently and slowly into a small circle on one end. Tie and allow to dry (L).

SPECIAL EFFECTS

Half a whisk broom or a portion of broom straw tied together.

Navaho Drum Rattle from Jingle Bells and Rattles, page 54.

OTHER MALLETS

See mallet suggestions for Wooden Xylophones, page 92.

Quick and Simple

1. Coffee cans with plastic lids. Remove metal bottom for a better sound. Paper covering the outside of the can may be decorated by children (A).
2. Small nut cans with plastic lids make nice bongo drums (B).
3. Oatmeal boxes and salt boxes are also "instant drums" (C).
4. Paper ice cream containers (the two-gallon size).
5. Pottery jars, flower pots or heavy metal kettles (D). Tie on a head of light 100% cotton canvas. Dampen. This will shrink and give a drumlike sound.

6. Wooden mixing or salad bowl with fabric thumbtacked over opening for a head (E).

HINTS

Broken tops of professional band drums make excellent heads for the smaller drums. Ask a drummer friend to save them for you.

The metal straps used around packing crates (and by plumbers) may be used to keep a drumhead tight.

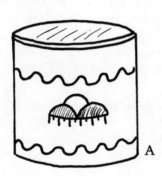

A

B

C

D

E

Zithers, Banjos and Dulcimers

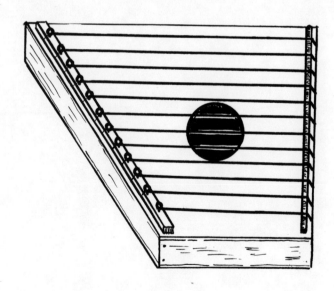

History

The oldest stringed instrument in the world is pictured on a cave wall in southern France. The artist lived about 15,000 B.C. The instrument is a hunting bow (without an arrow) held to the mouth of a strangely dressed man who is dancing toward a pair of bison. Musical vibrations and magic songs were thus paired in a primitive struggle for existence.

The sounds of vibrating strings have been used in all climates and all countries to help man face the problems of life and death. In the cold birch forests of the north of Finland, the legendary hero Vainamoinen made his kantele from the head of a giant fish and sang to wild animals and men. Near the sunny Mediterranean, Orpheus used his lyre to persuade the Greek gods to bring his wife back from the shades of death. On an Israeli desert a shepherd named David was summoned with his harp to the bedside of a restless king. And in our own country, the songs and guitars of youthful protestors helped stir a nation's conscience.

The material and shape of each stringed instrument are supplied by the culture, but the principle is the same. A string vibrates to make a sound when it is plucked, tapped or bowed. When the string is short the tone is high; when the string is long the tone is low. If the string is vibrated over a resonating chamber the tone becomes louder and changes in character (timbre) according to the shape and construction of the chamber.

The developmental histories of many instruments make fascinating stories. An example of this is the evolution of the present day bass fiddle. Centuries ago, in Africa, hunters commonly used a small animal trap that was made from a hole in the ground, covered by a skin. Stretched between the skin and a nearby bush was a thin, taut sinew. One day a hunter, with the innate inventiveness of the human species, recognized the musical possibilities, brought the idea home, and called it a ground bow. This same instrument is still played in Uganda and other African countries. The musician sits beside the skin-covered hole and plucks the string, which is held tight by a green stick planted nearby.

Later, in the eighteenth century, the Africans were forced into slavery on the American continent, and they needed music to ease their misery. So they re-created the old instrument in a more portable form and called it a washtub bass. When the drawing rooms of the plantation mansions began to receive European string groups, the servants recognized a new instrument. Using techniques of the old ground bow, they converted the slow symphonic dignitary, the bass violin, into a rhythmic jazzy folk instrument.

Stringed instruments have some advantages over other instruments. They are usually light and easy to carry. The development of the fingerboard makes it possible to change the length of the strings and makes the sound adaptable for solo or accompaniment. The sound box may be made any shape—triangular for a Russian balalaika, round for a banjo, or pear-shaped for a guitar. It may even be made from a gourd or an armadillo shell.

Most stringed instruments are plucked with a finger or a small plectrum made from a quill or a bone. A few are hammered like the piano, but a large number are bowed. Using a bow makes the vibrations long and steady, similar to the human voice. It is to the bowed strings that the standard music text usually refers when it classifies an instrument as a string, wind or percussion type.

On the American continent there were no stringed instruments except for the use of the hunting bow as a mouth bow by the California Indians. When the Spanish arrived in Mexico they introduced the violin. The Southwest Apache Indians made their own one-stringed version with a hollow wood branch.

The Appalachian dulcimer comes closest to being a real American folk instrument. It is used for both singing and dancing. Early mountain settlers from the British Isles adapted it from several sources. In The Dulcimer Book, *Jean Ritchie discusses in detail the history and use of this instrument. An authentic dulcimer is relatively easy to make and there are many instruction books and kits available. (See References.) The version in this book is even more simplified than most.*

There is a special quality found in stringed instruments. They are often difficult to play, but once they are mastered, they are especially satisfying to the musician. For the one who plays and the one who listens we might class this as a phenomenon that somehow touches the heart strings!

Mouth Bow

Granddaddy of all stringed instruments, the mouth bow has been played from 15,000 B.C. to the present day. The Appalachian folk play it; young popular recording artists play sophisticated versions.

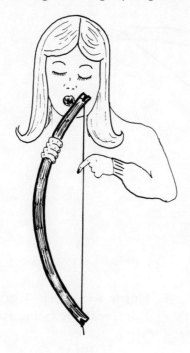

MATERIALS

1 yardstick (or similar piece of wood)
Nylon fishing line, 50-lb. test (safest for children), or a thin steel guitar string
Pocketknife
Bead (optional)

TO MAKE

1. With the pocketknife, make a notch in each end of the yardstick—a "V" shape about ½" long (A).
2. Make 2 more small notches with the pocketknife—one about 1" down from each side of one end of the yardstick. Make these in a "V" shape also (B). These notches will hold the nylon string tightly.
3. Measure string about 34" long. Attach string by looping it around the side notches and then bringing it up and through the end notch (C).
4. Slip on a bead, or make a large knot, at the other end of the nylon line. Slip the string over the other end of yardstick and pull the line taut (D). This will give a bow to the yardstick (E). The tautness of the string determines the tone, so adjust it as you wish.

TO PLAY

Play in the same manner as the Jew's harp: Hold the end of the wooden bow against partially opened, tensed lips. The shape of the mouth is changed to make a faint melody that contrasts with the louder drone of the plucked string. Pluck the string rhythmically with a fingernail, guitar pick, or small triangle cut from a plastic lid.

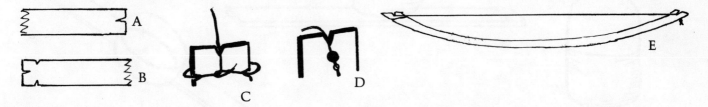

Birimbau

A bow with a gourd resonator from Brazil, this instrument originated in Africa. Our simple version uses plastic, which is easier to come by in our climate than gourds.

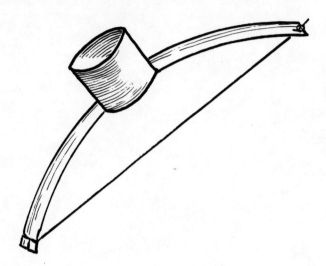

MATERIALS

Mouth Bow—see preceding page for the construction
1 round plastic gallon jug
Pencil or small stick for striking string
1 small screw
Screwdriver
Knife for cutting jug

TO MAKE

1. Make a Mouth Bow following instructions for Steps 1–3 on preceding pages.
2. With the knife, cut the bottom half from the plastic jug (A).
3. Center the bottom half of the jug on the yardstick (B).
4. Attach the jug to the yardstick with a screw (C).

5. Finish with Step 4 of Mouth Bow instructions, with jug facing away from string.

TO PLAY

This is primarily a rhythm instrument. The wooden stick (originally an arrow) is used to tap out rhythmic patterns. Hold the resonator on the abdomen if dancing or on the chest if sitting.

HINTS

A dance troupe from Brazil gives a striking exhibition with this instrument: it is played by dancers who create their own music as they dance.

For a science class, the addition of the plastic jug to the wooden bow gives a remarkable demonstration of a sound box.

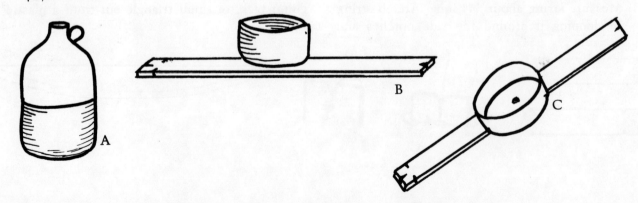

Cornstalk or Bamboo Fiddle

Very little tone, but it's fun to make and play. In Nigeria, eight or ten
bamboo stalks are laced together to make a zither.

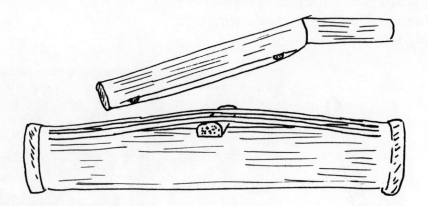

MATERIALS

Dry cornstalk or dry bamboo stalk
Sharp jackknife
Rosin as used on violin bows
Glue

TO MAKE

1. Select a large, strong section from the base of the stalk.
2. Cut a section from cornstalk leaving a node at each end (A).
3. In the center section, cut away the stalk from under the deep grooves so that two "strings" remain attached at both ends (B).
4. Cut a small bridge from an unused section of the stalk (cut the section in half lengthwise— C) and insert it gently under the strings (D).

5. For the bow, select a long section from the thinner end of the stalk. Cut it, leaving the end section intact, and leaving a 4" piece of the next joint for a handle (E).
6. Hollow out under one "string" only.
7. Cut two small bridges and insert near ends of the bow string (F).
8. Rub rosin on both the fiddle and the bow.

TO PLAY

Hold fiddle in left hand against collar bone. The fingers may be used to change the tone. Bow is held in the right hand—with care.

HINT

Now you can make like a scarecrow on Halloween!

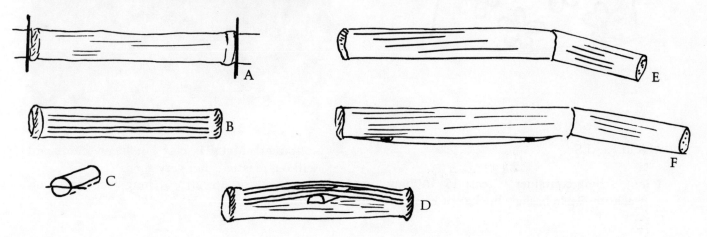

Washtub Bass

It was in San Francisco, the washtub bass was painted with blue for-get-me-nots, and the young street musician was busily "tuning" four guitar pegs on the broom handle. I leaned over and asked in astonishment what he was doing. He smiled jauntily and said with a big wink, "Pure facade, lady, pure facade."

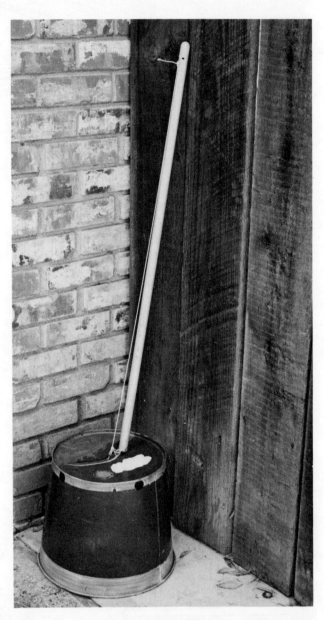

MATERIALS

1 large strong container at least 15″ in diameter (washtub, wastebasket, bucket or similar type container). Metal is best but heavy cardboard will do; plastic is not very good.

Broomstick (or dowel) 36″ long (depending on your height)

Strong cord (nylon is best), 48" long
⅜" eye bolt, washer and nut
Saw
Hammer and large nail
Drill

TO MAKE

1. With the saw, make a notch in one end of the broom handle to fit the bottom rim of the bucket (A).
2. Drill a hole through the other end of the broom handle, 2" down from the top (B).
3. With the hammer and nail, make a hole in the center of the bucket (C).
4. Insert eye bolt from the top; screw on washer nut from underneath (D). (If you are in a hurry, just tie the string over a small peg and draw it up through the hole in the tub).
5. Tie one end of the cord through the eye bolt.
6. Place notched stick on edge of tub. Put other end of cord through the hole in the broomstick. Slant the stick inward, pull cord tight and tie. You need good tension to make the tone.

TO PLAY

Place right foot on the bucket (this is to hold it down while strumming). Hold the end of the broomstick with the left hand, leaving the right hand free for strumming. The high and low tones are made by moving the stick back and forth, which tightens or loosens the string. You may also use your left fingers to change the tone. The note you play is customarily the bass note of the chordlike oom-pah of the tuba. Rhythmic strumming is very important.

HINT

With practice this can be a real instrument. One student told me, "Our band didn't have any money, so we used a washtub until we could buy a bass fiddle."

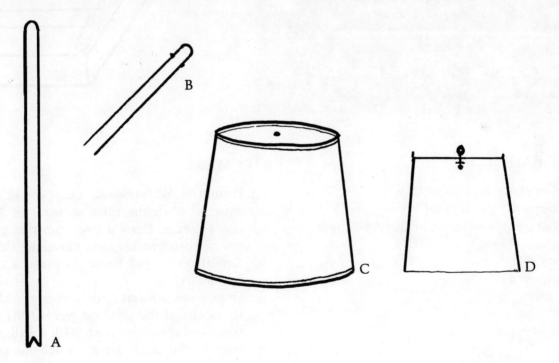

Zither (Psaltry)

Over 4,000 years ago, a Chinese emperor stretched five strings over a slightly curved board and made a "chin." He believed it would curb evil. Our representative from the large family of zithers has a simple box resonator. It may be made, however, without the box and with just a plain square of wood. The square wood version can be made by small children. Just follow the second half of the directions and omit the dowel for simplicity.

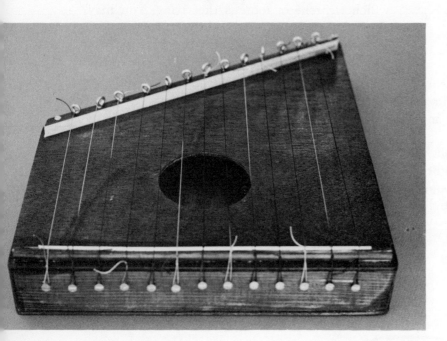

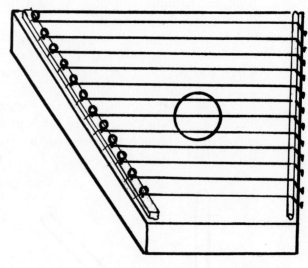

MATERIALS

1 piece of plywood, 28" x 14" x ⅛"
1 piece of pine, 1" x ¾" x 28"
Dowel or piece of pine, 24" long and ⅜" thick
12 screws, ⅝" long
12 screw eyes
Nylon fishing line
White glue
Screwdriver
Coping saw
Drill
Sandpaper
Stain or shellac (optional)
Pencil
Ruler

TO MAKE

1. From the ⅛" plywood, cut two 12" x 14" squares. With the ruler measure in 7" from one 14" edge. Draw a line from this point to one opposite corner, and cut along this line. Repeat on second board, to make a top and bottom (A).

2. Draw a circle about 3" in diameter in the center of one of the plywood pieces (this will be the top of the sound box). With a drill, make a hole in the circle large enough for the saw blade to slip through (B). Insert blade, attach it to saw and cut around the penciled line. Sand edges.

3. With the saw, cut 2 strips of ⅛" plywood,

each 1¾″ wide: 1 strip 14″ long and 1 strip 7″ long, to fit the sides of the box. Glue in place (C).

4. When glue is dry, cut 2 strips of ¾″ pine to fit the inside of the open ends of the box. Measure as you go to achieve a better fit. This heavy wood is best for holding screws and strong enough for the nylon fishing line. Glue in place and dry thoroughly (D). Sand the edges of the box.

5. From the ⅜″ dowel or ⅜″ square piece of wood, cut 2 pieces to fit across the top of the box. (These fit over the ends of the box where the ¾″ wood has been placed.) Glue in place (E). Dry thoroughly.

6. With a ruler and pencil, mark the placement of the screws on the 12″ edge of the box (F). Space the screws evenly across the side of box and about ½″ down from the top (F). Attach screws and screw in until about ¼″ of the head is protruding. Stain or shellac at this stage (optional).

7. With a ruler and pencil, mark on the opposite piece of dowel placement for the screw eyes (G). This can be a little tricky because of the slant of the wood. Measure from the screws already attached; this will give you a straight line. Drill holes in the dowel at each marking and attach screw eyes.

8. From the nylon fishing twine, cut each string 4″ longer than the distance between the screw and screw eye. Tie a loop in one end of the string and slip it over the screw on the side of the box, pull to the screw eye directly opposite and tie in a knot (H). Twist the screw eye for tuning. Continue in this manner until all the strings have been attached.

HINT

See the chapter on teaching methods for a way of using this instrument for teaching music reading to all ages.

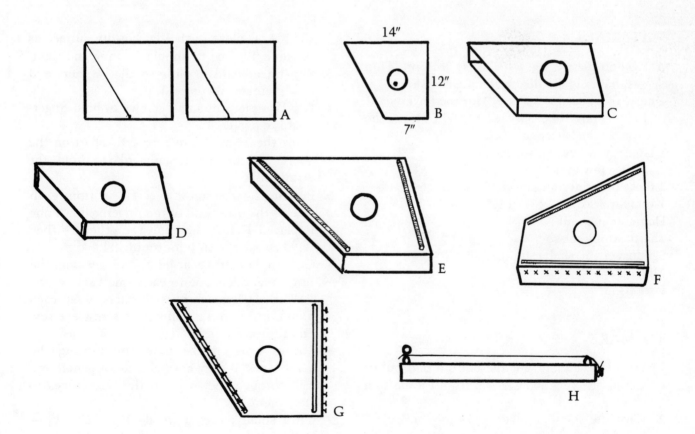

Plastic Bottle Banjo

The banjo sound box is open on the bottom. It has been made in the past from fence posts, cigar boxes and cookie tins, so our plastic jug is not too far out of line. If you wish, it is possible to upend it, get a violin bow and play this creation like a cello.

MATERIALS

A 1-gallon plastic jug, with a flat bottom. (Thin jugs that hold distilled water are good.)
1 piece of wood, 30″ x 2″ x ¾″, for the fingerboard
Nylon fishing line (at least 25-lb. test—the stronger the better)
2 large screw eyes for tuning pegs
2 small screw eyes
2 tacks or screws for holding jug to fingerboard
Wood for bridge, 1″ x ½″ x ½″
Hammer and nail
Sharp, strong scissors
Sandpaper and shellac (optional)
Pliers
Pocketknife

TO MAKE

1. With the scissors, cut the bottom half out of the plastic jug, about 5″ up from the bottom (A).
2. With the scissors, make slots for the fingerboard to slide through, on opposite sides of the jug, as close to the flat bottom surface as possible (B). The fit should be snug and tight.
3. Slip fingerboard in slots so that a short end (1¼″) remains on one side (C).
4. Use two tacks or small screws to hold fingerboard to jug (D).
5. Place the 2 small screw eyes ¾″ apart on the short end of the fingerboard, to hold the strings (E).
6. Put the 2 large screw eyes ⅝″ in from each side of the other end of the fingerboard. If one is placed 1″ from end and the other 2″, they will be easier to turn for tuning (F).
7. Cut 2 nylon strings at least 4″ longer than the fingerboard. Tie one to each small screw eye. Pull the string tightly with pliers, wrap each around the corresponding large screw eye several times, and tie.
8. Strings can now be tuned by turning the screw eyes. If they are tight, use a pencil or a nail through the loops in the screw eyes to turn them.
9. On a small piece of wood—1″ x ½″ x ½″—make grooves, using a pocketknife, ¾″ apart

for a bridge (G). Glue this bridge in place between the center of the jug and the small
screw eyes.

TO PLAY

Hold like a regular banjo, with left hand around
fingerboard and the sound box off to the right
side. The right hand strums near the sound box.

HINTS

Tune as you like. One way is to tune in fifths
(five notes apart) like a violin. Another way of
tuning is related to the dulcimer and the balalaika—the two strings are tuned to the same
note. Play the tune on only one string. Leave the
other string open, as a drone string.

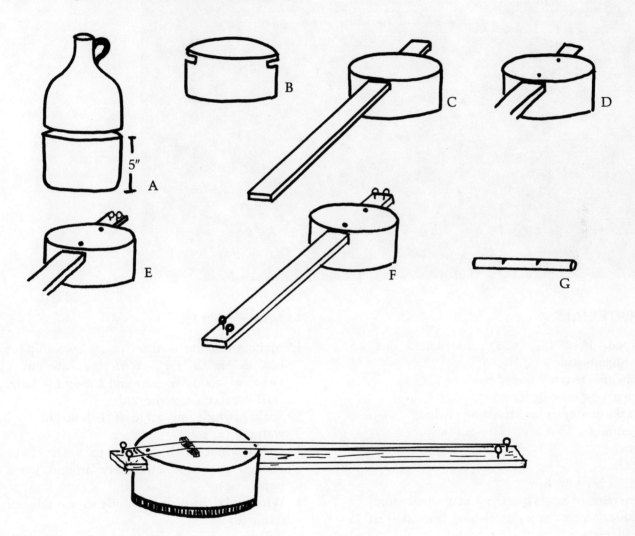

Rawhide Violin

*Bowed instruments need not resemble a Stradivarius violin. Invent
your own and you won't play second fiddle to anyone!*

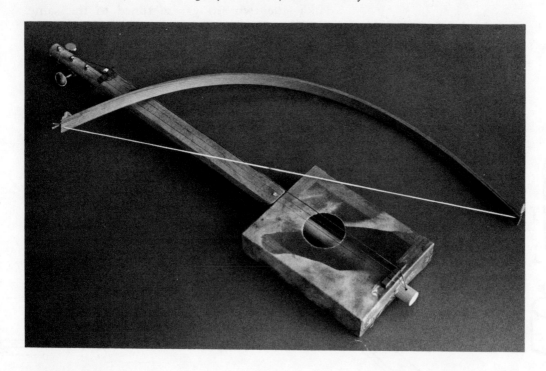

MATERIALS

Wood, 1" x 1¾" x 38", for sound box and
   fingerboard
Rawhide to cover sound box
8 nails for making frame
Tacks or staples for attaching rawhide
Hammer
Saw
Drill
26" of ⅝" dowel
3 machined heads (purchase at a music store)
Guitar strings or nylon fishing line (at least 25-
   lb. test)
Knife
Hardwood for bridges: one ¾" x ¼" x 1¼"; one
   1⁄16" x ¼" x 1¼".
1 piece of wood, 28" x ¼" x ½", for bow
1 spool 100% cotton thread for bow strings
Pencil
Rosin
2 screws

TO MAKE VIOLIN

1. Make a box out of the 1" x 1¾" wood. (Our
   box is 7½" x 5½".) With the saw cut 2
   pieces of wood 7½" long and 2 pieces 4" long.
   Nail the frame together (A).
2. Soak rawhide for at least 1 hour in cool
   water, until soft.
3. Cut rawhide with scissors to a size large
   enough to wrap completely around wood
   frame.
4. With tacks, hammer rawhide to one edge of
   frame (B).
5. Pull rawhide completely around frame and,
   overlapping first row of tacks and pulling
   tightly, tack in place (C).
6. Cut a corner out of the rawhide so that the
   edge will lie flat (D). Fold over frame and
   tack in place.
7. With a drill and ⅝" bit, drill a hole centered
   through each of the narrow ends of the box.
   With a knife, cut a sound hole in the raw-

hide about 3″ in diameter, 3″ from one end and centered between the sides (E).

8. Cut the ⅝″ dowel to a 26″ length and insert it through the holes in the box, leaving 1″ at one end for attaching the strings (F).

9. Cut a piece of wood 1″ x 1¾″ x 14″ for the fingerboard. Drill hole on each end of fingerboard. Center board on dowel, with one end against sound box. With pencil, mark position of fingerboard holes on dowel. Remove board; drill holes in dowel to match those in fingerboard. Drill holes the size of the machined heads in dowel, at end above fingerboard. Screw fingerboard in place. Insert machined heads (G).

10. Drill a hole in the dowel at the opposite end of the fingerboard and insert all three strings. If necessary, knot ends (H).

11. From the hardwood make two bridges, one 1⁄16″ x ¼″ x 1¼″, the second ¼″ x 1¼″ wide x ¾″ in the center slanting to ½″ on the sides. With a knife (or file), make 3 evenly spaced notches on the top of each bridge (I). Glue arched bridge on the rawhide box near the string end and the other bridge at the end of the fingerboard near the machined heads (see diagram). Dry thoroughly.

12. Place strings over bridges and attach to machined heads, making sure that the strings go over the sound hole.

TO MAKE BOW

13. Take the 28″ x ¼″ x ½″ piece of wood and cut a notch in the center of each end.

14. Measure 50 bow lengths of cotton thread. Tie together in a knot in one end and slip through notch in bow. Bend the bow (to measure length), make a knot in the other end of the cotton thread and slip through notch (J). The string should be taut. Use rosin on the bow.

TO PLAY

Hold the violin against your left upper arm, tuck it under your chin, or hold it between your knees. The left hand fingers the strings and the right hand holds the bow.

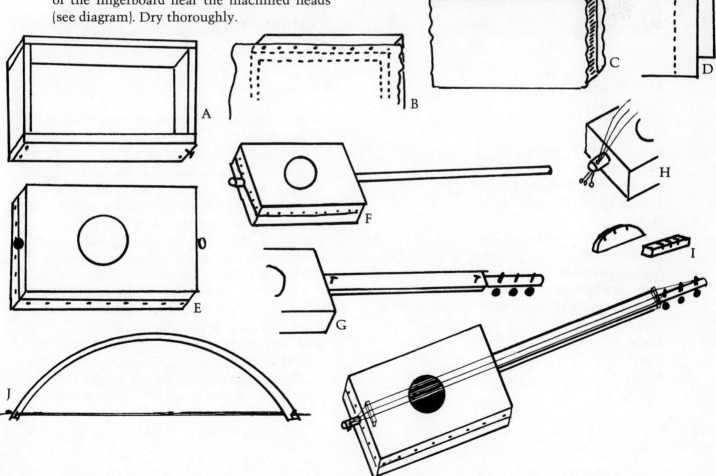

Appalachian Dulcimer

This truly American folk instrument was a favorite of the settlers in the Southern mountains. It has recently become very popular with folk singers because it is easy to play and can be used for singing accompaniments or for dancing.

Our three-stringed version is a simple primitive type. The standard hourglass shape is replaced by an easy-to-construct box. The fingerboard is small, but the techniques of playing are similar to those of a modern dulcimer.

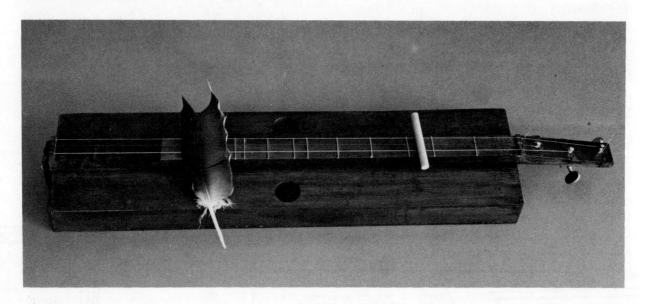

MATERIALS

⅛" plywood, 18" x 23"
White glue
Saw
Coping saw
Hardwood for bridges: one 1¼" x 1¼" x ¼"; one ⅛" x 1¼" x ¼"
Drill
Birch or other hardwood, 1¼" x ¾" x 28", for fingerboard
3 small screws for attaching strings
3 dulcimer strings or banjo strings (see below)
3 guitar machined heads (from the music store)
Wire for frets
File
Stain
Pencil
Plastic tape

TO MAKE

1. With the saw, cut two 6"-wide x 23"-long pieces out of the ⅛" plywood. On one of the plywood pieces mark four circles 1" in diameter 7½" in from each end. The outer edge of each circle should be ½" from the edge of the plywood (A). Cut out the circles with a coping saw; these are the sound holes.

2. Out of the remaining ⅛" plywood, cut 2 strips, each 23" x 1½". These are the sides of the box. Glue in place to top and bottom. Cut 2 more strips of ⅛" plywood, 1½" x 5¾", for the ends of the box. (To assure a good fit, measure as you go.) Glue in place.

3. Take the 1¼" x ¾" x 28" piece of birch (fingerboard) and measure 5" from one end. With the saw, taper from the ¾" height there to ½" at the end of wood (B). This is the end of

the fingerboard the machined heads will be attached to.

4. Measure 1½" from the other end of fingerboard; with the saw make a 4" shallow "U" shape (C). This is the strumming hole.

5. Cut 2 bridges out of the hardwood, one 1¼" x 1¼" x ¼", the second ⅛" x 1¼" x ¼" (D).

6. Glue the fingerboard in the center of the box, ¼" from one end. This is where the 1¼" x 1¼" x ¼" bridge is glued to box and fingerboard (E).

7. Take a piece of hardwood 1¼" x 2⅝" x ⅜" and glue it on the end of the box, against the bridge (E). We used the "U" shape from the strumming hole for this. This is for attaching the screws for strings.

8. Take the smaller bridge (1¼" x ⅛" x ¼") and glue it onto the fingerboard at the point where the fingerboard starts to taper (E, F). Let the glue dry thoroughly.

9. With the drill, make 3 holes the size of the small screws, evenly spaced on the 1¼" x 2⅝" x ⅜" wood at the end of the sound box (G). Then screw the 3 small screws in place, leaving about ⅛" of each head protruding so that the strings can be looped over them.

10. This is the best time for staining and finishing your instrument.

11. Frets must be placed according to the sound of each individual instrument. The illustration on the next page gives the *approximate* placement. Use plastic tape for markers until you find the exact spot. Painted lines are easiest; however, metal frets made from large paper clips may be added. Cut wire to fit the fingerboard, file a small groove in the board, add glue and wire.

12. With a drill, make 3 holes the size of the necks of the machined heads. (See H for placement.) Insert heads through holes and attach to bottom with screws (these come with the machined heads).

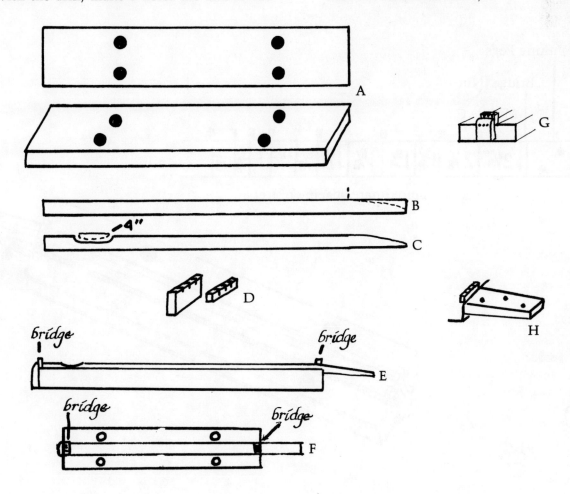

13. Use banjo strings—#2, #3, and #4 wound, medium gauge. You may also use dulcimer strings.

TO PLAY

Hold the instrument on your lap or on a table, with the tuning pegs to your left. Tune the strings five notes apart. The string farthest from you is C (Banjo #4), an octave below middle C. The middle string is G below middle D (Banjo #3). The string nearest you is middle C (Banjo #2).

Strum the strings with the right hand. Traditionally a turkey quill (cut like a pen) was used,

but you can cut a regular pick from a plastic lid. The melody is played on the nearest string by the left hand. You may use your finger or you may use a small wooden noter (3″ dowel). Strings 2 and 3 are drone strings. They usually remain the same and give a bagpipe-like accompaniment.

There are other ways of playing the dulcimer, and other tunings you may want to use. There are excellent books with directions for playing and directions for making the more complicated dulcimer. There are also many dulcimer kit manufacturers. Jean Ritchie's book provides excellent history and background, and *World Folk Songs*, by Marais & Miranda, gives songs to play as well as how to make and play the dulcimer. (See References.)

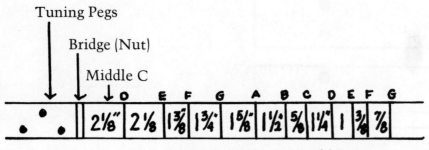

Approximate spacing of frets

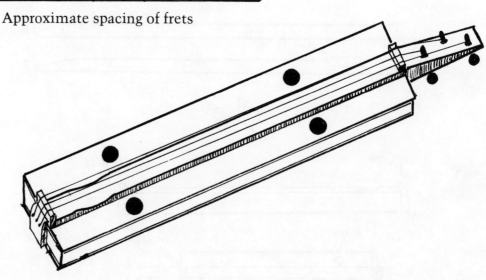

Gourd Mandolin

The gourd shape forms a natural resonating chamber.

MATERIALS

1 dry gourd, long and oval-shaped
8 screw eyes, for anchoring strings
Nylon fishing line, for strings
Dowel for a bridge, about ¼" x 3"
Triangular file
Knife for cutting sound hole

TO MAKE

1. Select a gourd that is long and narrow. On the flattest side of the gourd, cut a sound hole ⅓ of the way from the oval end (A).
2. With a spoon or your hand, clean out gourd, removing all the seeds and membrane. Dry thoroughly.
3. Attach four screw eyes, evenly spaced, at each end of the gourd. Leave enough space at the stem end for holding, and make sure the strings will cross the sound hole (B).
4. Tie strings to screw eyes, pulling tightly.
5. Using triangular file, make 4 evenly spaced grooves on dowel. Place grooved dowel under the strings for a bridge.

TO PLAY

Play like a guitar or mandolin by fingering with the left hand and strumming with the right hand over the sound hole.

Try tuning the four strings (twist the screw eyes) like bugle notes and play taps, reveille or other bugle calls.

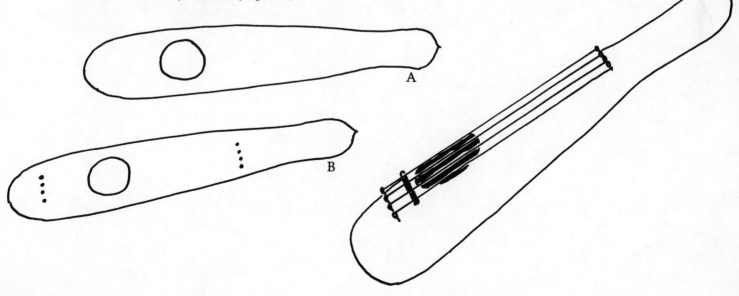

Quick and Simple

1. Small boxes, gift boxes, stationery boxes with a sound hole cut in the top. Stretch different sizes of rubber bands around the box and over the hole (A). Notice the different tones that come from each box with the various bands.
2. Same type of boxes. Use two pencils for bridges (B). When the strings are free along their vibrating length, they sound better.
3. Musical saw (C). Use a saw and a violin bow.

It takes practice and strength to play. Sit down and hold the handle of a long flexible saw tightly between feet, with the saw teeth facing body and the blade curved. With bow in left hand, lightly stroke the outside, smooth edge of the saw. Change the curve in the saw to change the note. The tighter the curve, the higher the note.

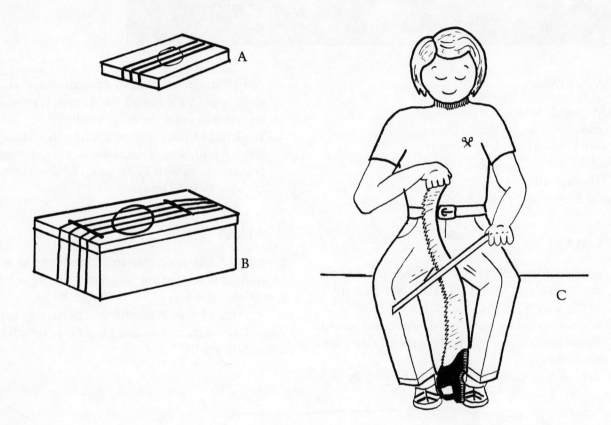

Flutes, Whistles and Horns

History

We often use the words life *and* breath *as if they were synonyms. Human emotions and experiences link them together, along with related words such as* wind *and* voice. *The wind is often referred to as a live being—we use phrases such as "blustering north wind" and "sighing breezes." Ghost stories refer to a cold draft that signals the presence of an unwanted spirit. It is no wonder that there are many superstitions about wind instruments.*

History and folk tales give many examples of unusual happenings with flutes and horns. The Pied Piper's flute cast a fatal spell on the rats and children; the protective powers of a magic flute inspired a Mozart opera; and scripture states that the Angel Gabriel will blow his trumpet to signify the final day of judgment.

The human voice is a wind instrument, and the metal piece beyond the lips is a further addition to the performer's speech. Because of the dynamic nature of the sound and because of the shape, horns have been considered masculine instruments. Trumpets proclaimed the crowning of kings even before the Roman legions, with their curved brass horns cornua, *marched across the known world during the early centuries* A.D. *The U.S. President is saluted by a Marine brass band. Soldier heroes are buried while a lone bugler sounds taps. In the Amazon jungles, Yanamamo women who accidentally see the giant flutes of the male coming-of-age ceremonies are quickly put to death.*

Religious ceremonies use wind instruments, too. The church pipe organ is a collection of many pipes. In Tibet, a special horn is made from the leg bone of a long-dead lama and reverently played at the beginning of the holy rites.

Wind instruments are usually divided into three categories: flutes, reeds and horns. A flute makes a soft hollow tone when air is blown across a hole in the end of the tube. It may be blown vertically across the open end or it may be held horizontally, the breath directed across a special hole. Whistles are related to flutes except that the air is channeled directly toward a sharp edge and the resulting tone is sharp and shrill.

Reed instruments, like the modern clarinet and oboe, have a flexible reed or reeds that vibrate. Children make reed instruments when they hold a blade of grass between their thumbs and blow.

The horn, named for its original material, gets its sound from the vibrations of the musician's lips. A small cup-shaped mouthpiece holds the lips firmly and the resulting sound is magnified by the shape of the instrument. The valves and slides of modern horns are elaborate ways of lengthening and shortening the metal tubes.

Like all other folk artifacts, there are many unusual variations of these wind instruments. Mountainous countries like Switzerland and

Tibet have developed huge horns for signaling across the valleys. The large calabash, or gourd flute, in Africa may have been the ancestor of the saxophone. The Eastern countries invented a leather bag to hold air so that their horns could play a constant sound. These bagpipes spread across Europe and found a special home in Scotland.

Horns are dramatic and exciting, and their sounds evoke strong emotions. Although modern brass instruments are very complex, there are many simple folk horns that are easy to make and to play.

Flute

Flutes may be played by blowing across the end (vertically) like the Japanese shakuhachi, but in the Western world they are most often blown horizontally through a hole on the side.

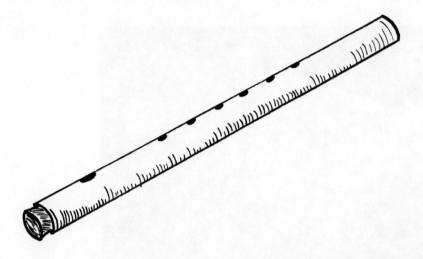

MATERIALS

1 tube—plastic, bamboo or wood. We used a
   snorkel ½″ in diameter and cut to the desired
   length.
Knife
Saw
Drill, with ³⁄₁₆″ bit, for the blowhole and the
   finger holes.
Round file
Cork to fit the end of the tube used

TO MAKE

1. Cut the tube the desired length—we used a
   12″ piece.
2. Insert cork in one end of the tube. If you are working with bamboo, leave a joint intact on one end, and smooth the remaining interior with sandpaper on a dowel.
3. Measure 1½″ from the closed end, and drill a ³⁄₁₆″ hole. With the file make the hole an oval about ³⁄₈″ across (A). This is the mouthpiece hole (blowhole).
4. With the ³⁄₁₆″ bit drill holes for the fingers: For a primitive, individualistic style, drill wherever your fingers fit; for a Western scale, follow pattern for recorder or Shepherd's Pipe (see page 149). File rough edges.

HINT

Mouthpiece size should vary according to the size of the tube.

A

Panpipes

The Greek god Pan loved a shy water nymph, who thwarted his advances by changing into a reed growing near the banks of the river. He made these pipes from the reeds and played them to soothe his lonely heart.

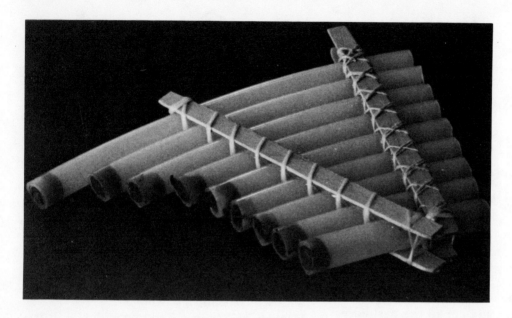

MATERIALS

41" of plastic tubing; firm plastic works best. (Bamboo or cornstalk will work well. Size may vary. We used plastic with an outside diameter of ½". Thin tubes make a thin sound. Larger tubes are more mellow.)
Knife
Clear plastic tape
Strips of bamboo or ice cream sticks for holding tubes together
String
Needle
Plasticine clay

TO MAKE

1. With a knife, cut the tube to the lengths you want. We used the measurements listed below for a C scale. These measurements are slightly long so that you can tune the pipes later.

C—6¾"	G—4¼"	D—3"
D—6"	A—3¾"	
E—5¼"	B—3½"	
F—4¾"	C—3¼"	

2. Place the cut plastic tubes side by side with the longest at one end and the smallest at the other (A). With tape, wrap the tubes together, making sure that the top edge is even for blowing (B).
3. Lay ice cream sticks or bamboo strips on top of tape, on both sides of tubes. Thread needle with string and tie the string to the angled pair of sticks. Sew back and forth between plastic pipe, catching the sticks on both sides. This holds the panpipes firmly in place. Now place the other two sticks straight across pipes. Repeat the above. Tie a knot (C).
4. Insert the clay in the ends of the plastic tubes, filling the end of each pipe until it makes the note you want. The clay can be pushed in further to make the pitch higher or lower.

TO PLAY

Holding panpipes in hand, blow across the open ends of the tubes.

HINT

These may be tuned to any scale you like. The longest pipe will be the lowest tone. You may also tune it to a Scottish or Chinese scale, or to one of the modes used in Appalachian songs—for example, "Old Joe Clark."

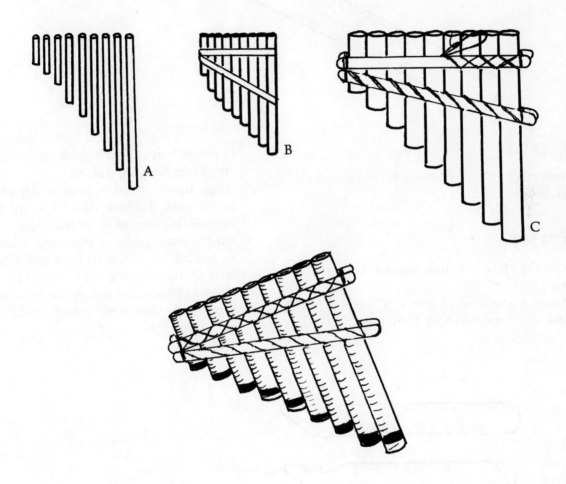

Spring Willow Whistle

This whistle is most easily made in the spring when the running sap makes the willow bark slip off easily. It is a favorite old-fashioned toy.

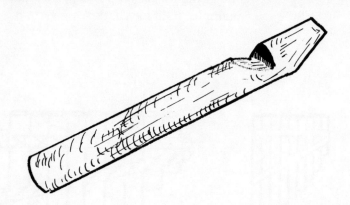

MATERIALS

4″ to 6″ piece of willow, about ⅝″ in diameter
Pocketknife

TO MAKE

1. Cut the piece of willow about 4″ long, making sure it is straight.
2. Make a small notch about ¼″ deep ½″ from one end. Starting about 1″ from end, according to size of branch, cut branch on a slant to first cut. Taper blowing end (A).
3. Using handle of knife, tap center of branch gently until the bark slips off in an unbroken tube (B). Dipping in water may help.
4. On the inner piece of wood, cut a long notch to within ½″ of the straight end. Cut a thin strip off the blowing end for an air passage (C).
5. Slide bark back and line up the notches.
6. Test by blowing; if the tone is poor, make the air strip wider.

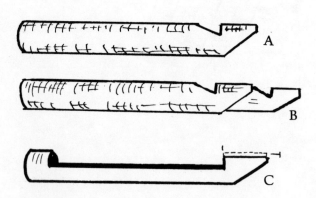

Bone Whistle

The Oglala Sioux used hollow bird bones to make the whistles for their famous Sun Dance, for what could come closer to Wakan-Tanka, the Sun God, than the giant eagle?

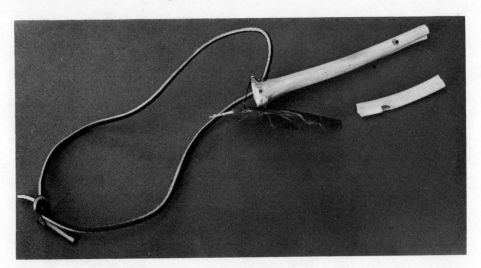

MATERIALS

Wing or drumstick of a turkey (raw)
Bleach or lemon juice
Small wood plug
Stiff wire, skewer or nutpick for hollowing bone
Coping saw
Knife
White glue

TO MAKE

1. Boil meat from bone (roasting often burns and crumbles the bone). Scrape the bone with a knife until clean. Use skewer or nutpick to hollow bone.
2. Boil or soak bone in bleach or lemon juice to whiten.
3. Saw ends from bone to give as long and straight a tube as possible (A).
4. Follow the directions for the Shepherd's Pipe (see page 149) to make whistle mouthpiece. Naturally you must adjust the size to suit the small bone.
5. One or two small finger holes may be drilled in a long bone if you desire.
6. A hole in the end of the whistle will hold a leather thong for your neck. Glue on a fluffy feather to respond to your breath.

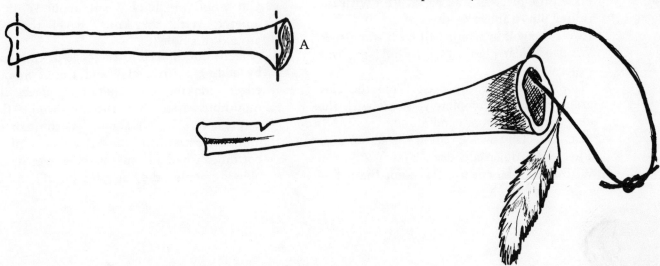

Ceramic Whistle

Fanciful creatures with voices.

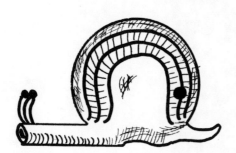

MATERIALS

Small package of self-hardening Mexican pottery
  clay
Rolling pin, dowel or tube for rolling clay
Medium size ball (tennis or golf)
Wax paper
Knife
Pencil

TO MAKE

1. Take a ball of clay about 2″ in diameter, and place on a piece of wax paper. Roll with the rolling pin to about ¼″ thickness.
2. Cover the golf or tennis ball with wax paper. We used clear plastic tape to hold the wax paper in place.
3. Place the ball on the clay. Wrap the clay around the ball completely. Work with the clay until it is smooth and round.
4. Place the clay-covered ball in the sun or near a heater until partially dry.
5. With the knife, cut the clay—not the ball—in half (A). Remove the plastic-wrapped ball from the center.
6. Place the two clay halves back together, making a sphere (B). Take more clay and carefully fill in the knife edge. Using water to thin the clay makes it more workable.
7. Take another piece of clay—about a 1″ ball— and make a round, long shape, 2″ long and ½″ in diameter (C). This is for the mouthpiece.
8. With a knife, make a flat hole through the center, down the length of the clay mouthpiece (D). This is to blow through.
9. Cut a hole in the clay ball, about ½″ in diameter. With the knife, bevel the edge around this hole (E).
10. Attach mouthpiece to the edge of this hole, by adding a little clay and water. Smooth edges, making sure not to squeeze the mouthpiece so that the air won't flow through it. The air should go through the mouthpiece and hit the ½″ air hole in the bottom of the ball—just passing over it, like blowing across the top of a jug (F). Adjust

mouthpiece for proper angle to make sound.

11. Make a hole in the side of the ball about ¼″ in diameter (G).

12. At this point, you may add a head, a tail or, with the pencil, make nice designs in the clay while it is still workable. When you have achieved your fanciful design, place the whistle in the sun or near a heater to dry.

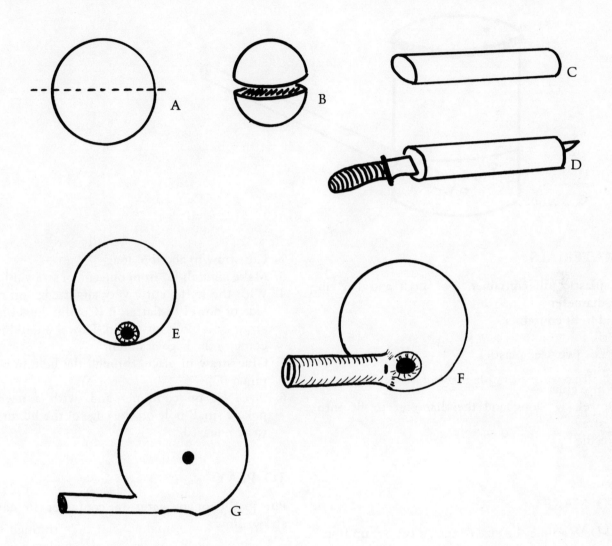

Water Whistle

This will remind you of a small bird high in the orange tree.

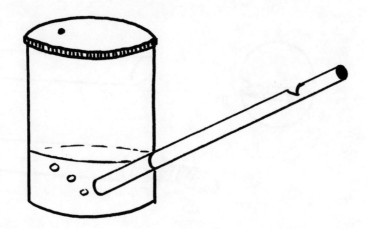

MATERIALS

1 plastic pill container, 2½" high and 1½" in
   diameter
Lid to fit container
Drill
Straw (we used plastic)
Knife
White glue
Dowel, ½" long and the diameter to fit into
   straw
Needle
Water

TO MAKE

1. Drill a hole the size of the straw, ½" up from
   the bottom of the plastic container (A).

2. Cut straw to about 5" long.
3. Make a notch ½" from one end of straw (B).
4. With the knife, cut a very slight edge off one
   side of dowel to flatten it (C). Slip dowel into
   straw and blow for sound. Dowel should just
   come to the edge of notch.
5. Glue straw in place, through the hole in container (D).
6. Place lid on container and, with a needle,
   poke a small hole on the edge of the lid for air
   to be released.

TO PLAY

Put just enough water in container to cover
straw. Blow.

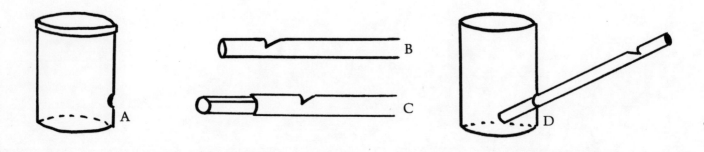

Shepherd's Pipe (Recorder type)

The gentle sound of this instrument entertained the shepherd and kept the sheep from wandering too far around the mountain. It is important to remember that the tone of the instrument comes from directing a strong stream of air against a sharp surface. Study the illustrations carefully and use a sharp knife on the air hole!

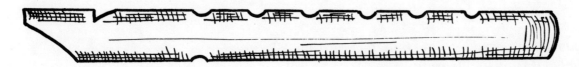

MATERIALS

Bamboo, 12" long and with at least a ⅝" inside diameter, or stiff plastic tube or garden hose
Cork or wood plug to fit inside the tube
Coping saw
Drill and ³⁄₁₆" bit
Small round file
Sharp knife
Pencil

TO MAKE

1. If you are using bamboo, clean and smooth the inside of the stalk.
2. Measure 1" from blowing end and cut an air hole ½" square. Note the sharp, slanting cut on one side (A).
3. Measure the cork or wood plug and cut it, if necessary, to make sure it ends just at the air hole in the bamboo. Cut a slanting air passage ³⁄₁₆" to ⅛" along the top edge of the plug (B). You may enlarge it later, but start small.
4. Insert plug in the end of the bamboo. Make sure that the air will blow against the sharp edge of the air hole (C).
5. Make the air passage a little larger if the sound is weak. Blow gently and keep trying—this is the hardest part.
6. Tune pipe to lowest note by sawing off the end ⅛" at a time—measurements should give a C scale going up from middle C.

7. To make finger holes, draw a straight line from middle of air hole to the far end of the pipe (D).
8. Mark the spot for each finger hole along this line, beginning 2" up from the end of the pipe (E). Notice that hole b is played on a hole *underneath* the top hole, which is c, an octave higher than the original note.
9. Drill a ³⁄₁₆" hole at hole c. Blow to test pitch. Raise the pitch by enlarging the hole slightly on the mouthpiece side. Lower the pitch by enlarging toward the open end.
10. Tune each note before drilling the next one. Work carefully, but if you make a mistake, put some cloth tape across part of the hole.

TO PLAY

Hold pipe with left thumb on hole b and three fingers above the pipe. The right hand has three fingers poised over the remaining holes. Blow gently. Place index finger of left hand on hole c, thus covering two holes. Then cover remaining holes consecutively, until all holes are closed. You will then have played a scale.

HINTS

You may wish to make the mouthpiece more comfortable by tapering it; make your cut starting ½" from the end (see diagram).

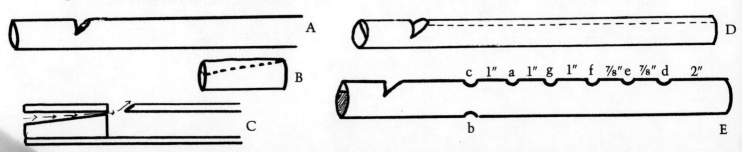

A

B

C

D

c 1" a 1" g 1" f ⅞" e ⅞" d 2"

b

E

Indian Love Flute

Comes a youth with flaunting feathers,
With his flute of reeds, a stranger
Wanders piping through the village,
Beckons to the fairest maiden,
And she follows where he leads her,
Leaving all things for the stranger.

　　　　Longfellow, Song of Hiawatha

The American Indian used his flute only for courting. The outside
wind channel is its unusual feature.

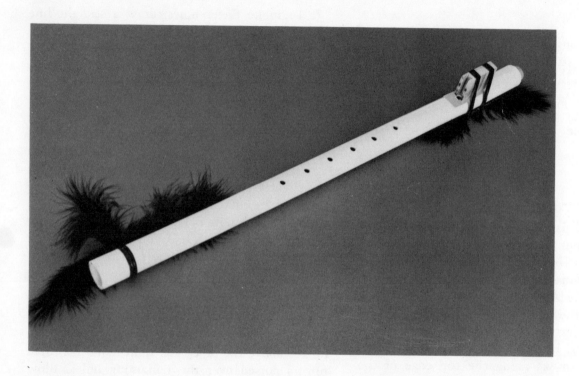

MATERIALS

1 piece of firm plastic 23″ long and ¾″ in diameter (sprinkler pipe is what we used)
1 plastic lid (e. g., a coffee can lid)
1 piece of hardwood, 1⅛″ x ⅜″ x 1⅞″
¾″ dowel, ¾″ long, to fit in plastic tube
Rubber bands, for testing tone
Posterboard for gasket, ⅛″ x ½″ x 1⅞″
Drill
Knife
File
Sandpaper

Glue (we used white glue and glue especially for plastic)
Saw
Leather thongs

TO MAKE

1. With a saw, cut 4″ from the end of the 23″ plastic tube (A).
2. Using a glue for plastics, glue the plastic lid to the 4″ piece of tube (B). Dry thoroughly.
3. Glue the 19″ piece of tube to the lid. Dry.

Cut the lid to just the diameter of the tubing. You now have a long tube with a plastic gasket to stop air flow (C).

4. With a drill and ¼" bit, space and drill holes as shown (D).

5. The first hole next to the plastic gasket on the longest piece of tubing should be beveled. This can be done by filing on the inside of the tube (E).

6. With the file or sandpaper, flatten the sound hole part of the flute, so that the posterboard gasket will lie flat (F).

7. Make a gasket out of the posterboard, cutting a piece ½" x 1⅞". Cut the center out of this, ¼" x 1⅛" (G). Glue over the two sound holes; don't cover them (H).

8. With the saw or knife, cut a ¼" groove on the 1⅛" edge of the 1⅛" x ⅜" x 1⅞" piece of hardwood (I). Sand smooth.

9. Drill a ⅛" hole in the center of the flat side of the ¾" x ¾" dowel for mouthpiece. Glue in the 4" end of tubing (J).

10. Slip the block of hardwood over gasket on the tube, with the ¼" groove facing the finger holes. Attach with rubber bands; shift the block back and forth to attain proper tone.

11. When the proper tone is achieved, tie the wood block in place with leather thongs to replace the rubber bands.

TO PLAY

Blow gently. Adjust the top piece until you get a tone.

HINTS

For a traditional appearance, you may carve the external air channel (hardwood block) and wrap a couple of leather thongs around your flute.

Traditionally, each Indian made his flute to fit his fingers. Then he composed his own songs on the flute. You may follow this individualistic pattern or you may make a Western scale on your flute by following the directions given for the Shepherd's Pipe (see page 149).

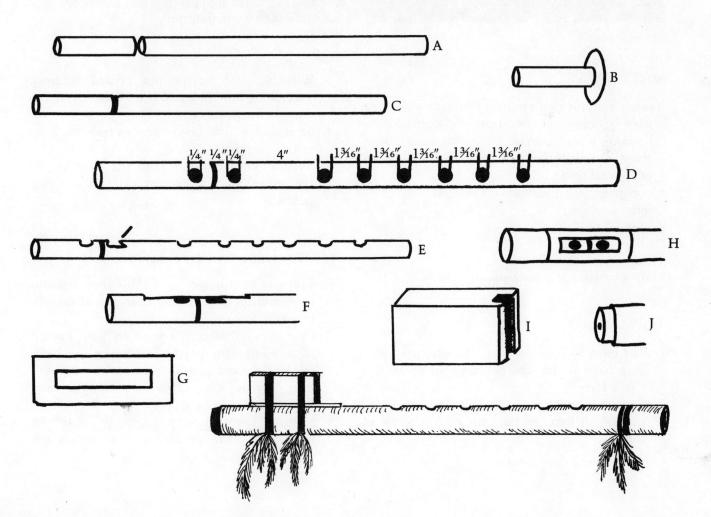

Horn Bugle

"Why don't you blow that ram's horn," Joshua said,
"'Cause the battle am in my hands."

From the spiritual *Battle of Jericho.*

Horn Bugle (top) and Conch Shell Horn (bottom).

MATERIALS

1 cow's horn (or ram's horn if you have one). You may be able to get one from a slaughterhouse or from a veterinarian. Craft shops may have them, although they may be plastic imitations of the real thing.
Mouthpiece (see directions for details)
Coping saw
Knife
Drill with ¼" bit
Sandpaper
Boiling kettle and camp stove

TO MAKE

1. Get horn as fresh as possible; otherwise you may have to set up the camp stove on the "back forty."
2. Cover horn with water and boil in a large kettle, for an hour or two, or until marrow is soft.
3. With a knife, scrape out center. Remove everything but the basic horn shell. Scrape to smooth rough edge.
4. Sand and polish inside and outside of horn with sandpaper.
5. Saw off sharp point of horn (A) according to the mouthpiece type you plan to use (see below).

MOUTHPIECE (THREE CHOICES):

6. Trumpet mouthpiece. Drill hole from tip into open portion of horn and insert metal mouthpiece (B).
7. Plastic mouthpiece. Remove the top from a large white glue bottle. Wash out the hardened glue. Sand screw top smooth so it won't hurt your lips. Clip off ¼" of point (C). Insert in hole drilled in horn.
8. Natural horn mouthpiece; horn must be thick. Saw off tip of horn at point where it is

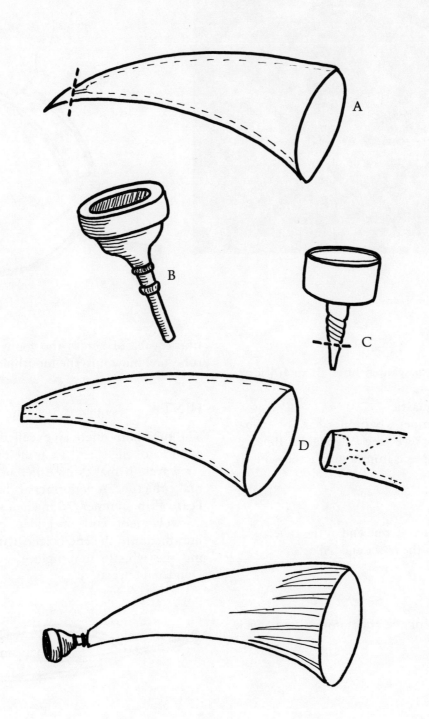

1″ in diameter. Solid horn material must extend at least one more inch beyond. Drill a hole ⅝″ in diameter and ⅝″ deep in the end of the horn. This hole may be larger but not smaller. Drill a ¼″ hole in the center of the ⅝″ hole that reaches to the open interior of the horn (D).

TO PLAY

Hold lips straight and tight and close together. Blow hard and the vibration of the lips in the small chamber will make a sound. You may blow one big blast or blow bugle calls of about five notes.

Plastic Tube Horn

Interesting and ridiculous.

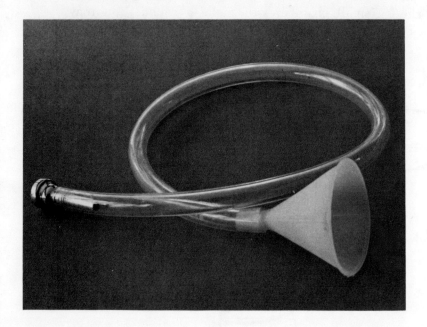

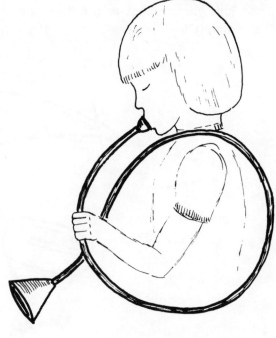

MATERIALS

Long plastic tube or garden hose, 2' to 10' long,
  as you wish
Funnel, metal or plastic
Mouthpiece—trumpet, baritone sax or tuba;
  whistle mouthpiece (see Shepherd's Pipe, p.
  149); or mouthpiece from a purchased whistle

TO MAKE

1. Place mouthpiece in one end of the tube.
2. Place funnel in the other end (A).

TO PLAY

Place the middle of the tube around your neck
like a tuba or across the room like a speaking
tube, and blow into the mouthpiece.

HINT

The tube horn offers an excellent demonstration
of some of the scientific principles of sound and
air waves. It makes no difference how long you
make the tube. A performer at the Wolf Trap Folk
Festival in summer '76 made a similar one from
a twelve-foot coil of gilded plastic pipe. He
hummed into the end (kazoo style) instead of using the whistle mouthpiece, and called it his
Duodenal Special.

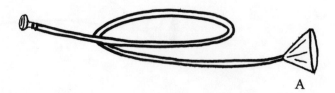

A

Slide Whistle

On an ornamental iron balcony in the French Quarter in New Orleans, Ilene saw an extraordinary band. The "trombone" player's instrument was made from a regular trombone mouthpiece, two pipes and a funnel. The bottom pipe had the funnel soldered to one end and it slid in and out of the first pipe. The music was marvelous!

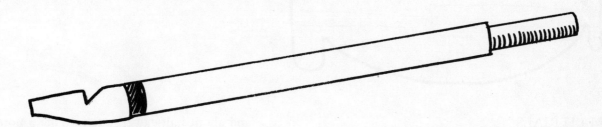

MATERIALS

(This is for a plastic one. If you want a metal pipe you are on your own.)

Plastic tube, about 12" (should be firm plastic)

Dowel, to fit the inside diameter of the plastic tube, 14" long

Felt or thin foam plastic

Whistle mouthpiece, purchased or constructed (see Shepherd's Pipe, page 149)

Fabric tape

Coping saw

White glue

TO MAKE

1. Cut tube to 12" long or desired length. You may even make your own tube from a sheet of plastic rolled around the dowel and fastened with clear plastic tape.

2. Attach whistle mouthpiece with fabric tape to one end of the plastic tube (A).

3. Place a small circle of felt or plastic foam on the end of the dowel; this should be glued to fit the end of the dowel near the mouthpiece so it will be airtight in the plastic tube (B).

TO PLAY

Blow gently and move slide in and out.

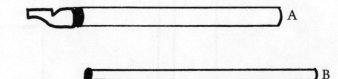

Wooden Animal Whistle

Another fanciful creature with a voice.

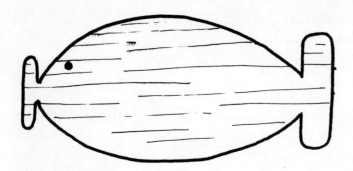

MATERIALS

1 piece of pine, 1½" x ¾" x 5"
Drill and ⅜" bit
Saw
½" of ⅜" dowel
Sandpaper

TO MAKE

1. With the drill and ⅜" bit, make a hole 3" deep in the end of the 5" piece of wood (A).
2. Saw ½" from the drilled end, into the hole and about halfway through. Make a notch ¾" from this cut to meet the original cut. This will give you a whistle hole (B).
3. Sand ⅓ of the rounded side of the dowel, or down enough to just meet the "V" in the whistle hole (C). Insert dowel (D) and test by blowing. If it doesn't whistle, sand a little more.
4. To make your animal, pick a shape you like and cut it from the wood, making sure you don't cut into the 3" hole drilled through the center.

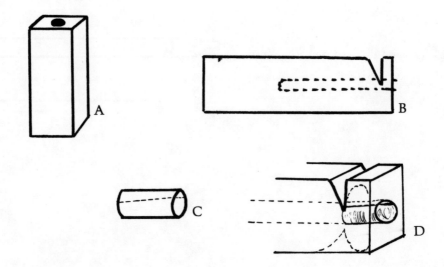

Unusual Variations

ANTARA

The panpipes of the Quechua Indians of South America were three and four feet long, with a deep sound.

DIDGERIDOO

The Australian aborigines use a hollow bamboo tube five to six feet long and two to four inches wide. A beeswax circle cushions the lips, which blow trumpet-fashion into the tube. The technique involves special breathing (like a glassblower) and continuous blowing with a rhythmic accent. Even in Australia a plastic pipe might replace bamboo.

DOUBLE PIPES

Two shepherd's pipes fastened together enable one musician to play two notes at a time.

BIRCHBARK HORN

In Finland, birchbark is rolled into a long cone shape. A trumpet mouthpiece is used. You can roll a brown plastic sheet, such as a notebook cover, into a horn-shaped cone.

CONCH SHELL

Saw one to three inches from the point until you can see the coils. Chisel out a cone-shaped mouthpiece. Drill a ¼" hole into the open interior of the shell. (See photo, page 152.) Blow hard and Triton himself will rise from the waves.

SEAWEED

Hollow tubular seaweed may be dried into a straight tube and blown with a trumpet mouthpiece.

PREDATOR WHISTLES AND ANIMAL CALLS

These are constructed in many ways. Check a sports store for ideas.

Quick and Simple

1. Humming comb. Place comb in a folded square of wax paper (A). Hum gently, with lips on wax paper, and your breath will vibrate the paper between your lips.
2. Cardboard kazoo. Cover one end of a cardboard tube with wax paper held by a rubber band or plastic tape (B). Hum loudly into open end with tube around mouth, so it will vibrate like a kazoo. Young children like to paint their horns.
3. Paper megaphone. Roll stiff paper into a cone shape; tape to hold (C). Sing through your "horn."
4. Plastic jug megaphone. Cut the top half off a large jug. Tie a tassel on the handle for extra class (D).
5. Water jugs. Use a "little brown jug," glass jug or bottle and blow across top edge of it. Tune by adding water (E). Try a scale with eight similar bottles, filled to various heights.
6. Panpipes. Take glass test tubes and tune by filling with water or clay (F).
7. Plastic drinking straws. Cut different lengths and blow like panpipes; or make a whistle using a small wood plug (see Spring Willow Whistle, page 144); or make an oboe or double reed whistle: Flatten two inches of straw at one end. Cut the end into two one-inch-long narrow tongues (G). Put the whole mouthpiece in your mouth and blow hard. Vary the length of your oboe or whistle to hear the changes in tone.

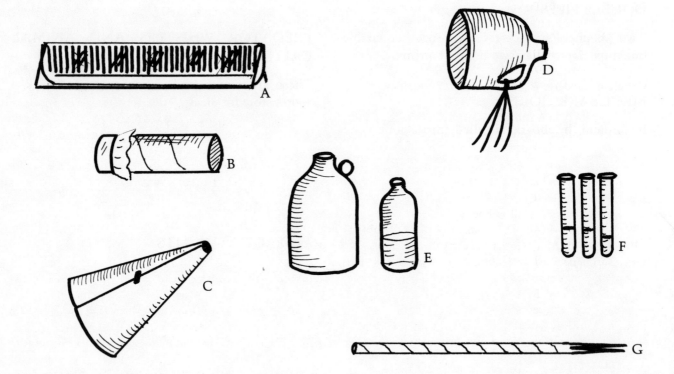

References

Baines, Anthony, ed., *Musical Instruments Through the Ages* (Baltimore: Penguin Books, 1961).

Bonanni, Filippo, *The Showcase of Musical Instruments* (New York: Dover Publications, 1964).

Boulton, Laura, *Musical Instruments of World Cultures* (New York: Intercultural Arts Press, 1972).

Buchner, Alexander, *Folk Music Instruments of the World* (New York: Crown Publishers, 1972).

Courlander, Harold, *Negro Folk Music, U.S.A.* (New York: Columbia University Press, 1963).

Curtis, Natalie, ed., *The Indian's Book* (New York: Dover Publications, 1968).

Densmore, Frances, *American Indians and Their Music* (New York: Womans Press, 1926; reprinted New York: Johnson Reprint Corp.).

———, *Music of the Maidu Indians of California* (Los Angeles: Southwest Museum, 1958).

Einstein, Alfred, *A Short History of Music* (New York: Vintage Books, 1954).

Elkin, A. P., and Trevor A. Jones, *Arnhem Land of Music* (Australia: Oceanic Monographs #9, December 1953).

Gelineau, R. Phyllis, *Songs in Action* (New York: McGraw-Hill, 1974).

Grunfeld, Frederic V., *Music* (New York: Newsweek, 1974).

Hellman, Neal, and Sally Holden, *Life Is Like a Mountain Dulcimer* (New York: Ludlow Music Inc., 1974).

Hofmann, Charles, *American Indians Sing* (New York: The John Day Co., 1967).

Hunt, Ben W., *The Complete How-To Book of Indian Craft* (New York: Collier Books, 1973).

Huskisson, Y., *Music of the Bantu* (Sovenga: Publications of University College of the North, 1969).

Ives, Burl, *The Burl Ives Song Book* (New York: Ballantine Books, 1953).

Jones, Bessie, and Bess Lomax Hawes, *Step It Down* (New York: Harper & Row, 1972).

Joseph, Joan, *Folk Toys Around the World and How to Make Them* (New York: Parent's Magazine Press, 1972).

Kendall, Alan, *The World of Musical Instruments* (New York: The Hamlyn Publishing Group Ltd., 1972).

Mandell, Muriel, and Robert E. Wood, *Make Your Own Musical Instruments* (New York: Sterling Publishing Co., 1957).

Marais & Miranda, *World Folk Songs* (New York: Ballantine Books, 1964).

Mason, Bernard S., *Drums, Tom Toms, and Rattles* (New York: Dover Publications, 1974).

Minor, Marz Nono, *The American Indian Craft Book* (New York: Popular Library, 1972).

Mitchell, Howard W., *The Mountain Dulcimer: How to Make It and Play It—After a Fashion* (Sharon, Ct.: Folk-Legacy Records, 1965).

Nettl, Bruno, *An Introduction to Folk Music in the United States* (Detroit: Wayne State University Press, 1962).

———, *Folk and Traditional Music of the Western Continents* (Englewood Cliffs, N.J.: Prentice-Hall, 1973).

Ritchie, Jean, *The Dulcimer Book* (New York: Oak Publications, 1972).

Roberts, Ronald, *Making Musical Instruments—Made to Be Played* (Woodridge, N.J.: Dryad Press, 1968).

Schnacke, Dick, *American Folk Toys—How to Make Them* (Baltimore: Penguin Books, 1974).

Seeger, Pete, *Steel Drums of Kim Loy Wong* (New York: Oak Publications).

Tobitt, Janet, *A B C's of Camp Music* (Pleasantville, N.Y.: Girl Scouts of America, 1955).

Weidemann, Charles C., *Music in Sticks and Stones* (New York: Exposition Press, 1967).

Whiteford, Andrew, *North American Indian Arts* (New York: Golden Press, 1970).

Williams, Peter, *Lively Craft Cards* (London: Mills and Boon Ltd., 1970).

WHERE TO BUY KITS

The Dulcimer Shoppe, P. O. Box 110, Mountain View, Arkansas 72560

Grey Owl–Indian Craft Manufacturing Co., 150–02 Beaver Road, Jamaica, New York 11433

Here Inc., 410 Cedar Avenue, Minneapolis, Minnesota 55454

The Hughes Company , 3665 West 13th Avenue, Denver, Colorado 80215

Within the last year many new companies have added musical instruments to their kit supplies.